P9-DWG-673

# Know Who You Believe

## The Magnificent Connection

## PAUL E. LITTLE

ww.cookministries.com/victor

Victor® is an imprint of
Cook Communications Ministries, Colorado Springs, Colorado 80918
Cook Communications, Paris, Ontario
Kingsway Communications, Eastbourne, England

KNOW WHO YOU BELIEVE
© 2003 by MARIE LITTLE

Original edition copyrighted © 1976 by Vision House Publishers, under the title *Faith Is For People*; revised edition by Marie Little, © 1987 under the title *The Answer to Life*.

All rights reserved. No part of this book may be reproduced without written permission, except for brief quotations in books and critical reviews. For information, write Cook Communications Ministries, 4050 Lee Vance View, Colorado Springs, Colorado 80918.

First Printing, 2003
Printed in the United States of America

1 2 3 4 5 6 7 8 9 10 Printing/Year 08 07 06 05 04 03

Editorial: John Conaway, Product Manager; Craig Bubeck, Sr. Editor
Cover & Interior Design: Image Studios

Unless otherwise noted, Scripture quotations are taken from the Holy Bible: New International Version. Copyright © 1973, 1978, 1984 by International Bible Society. Used by permission of Zondervan Publishing House. All rights reserved.

Library of Congress Cataloging-in-Publication Data

Little, Paul E.
  Know Who You Believe / Paul E. Little.
    p. cm.
Rev. ed. of: The answer to life. 1987.
  ISBN 0-7814-3815-2 (pbk.)
  1. Apologetics. 2. Christian life. I. Little, Paul E. Answer to
life. II. Title.
  BT1103 .L58 2003
  239--dc21

                                                    2002012324

**Publisher's Note:** Writers and publishers are often coached to "write as people speak" in order to best communicate with today's readers. Thus we have deliberately titled this book *Know Who You Believe* instead of using the grammatically correct—but awkward—*Whom*. Our apologies to purists everywhere.

# CONTENTS

# PREFACE

Do you question whether God knows or cares about you in your everyday life? Would you like to be connected with God? Do you feel you need to know a little more about God before connecting with Him? If so, this book is for you.

Like a fish to water, like an eagle to flying, my husband, Paul Little, gravitated to discussions with college and university students. In twenty-five years of lecturing on five continents, he never withdrew from getting into the ring to champion the Christian faith. He was known for his pithy one-liners: *"You don't have to kiss your brains good-bye to become a Christian"* ... *"God is not like a vending machine—put in a nickel and out comes a blessing"* ... *"God's love is more than you think. He uses information to help us to connect"* ... *"Physics cannot be learned from a telephone book. To find God, we need to look in the right place."*

Dispelling myths brought out the apologist in Paul; skeptics and doubters were welcomed. "We don't have to commit intellectual suicide to see the credibility of the Christian message."

One of Paul's frequently used fraternity talks started with this question, "What makes a person a Christian?" A friend of mine read this line and told me it immediately caught her attention. In a world where Oprah calls out, "Hope lives, prayer lives, love lives," I feel urged to quote Paul: "It does matter what we believe."

All the material in this book comes from the cache of Paul's files and tapes, starting with a previous book entitled *The Answer to Life*. Though it has been twenty-eight years since his earthly ministry abruptly ended in a head-on collision, the thoughts (and theology) are his. Therefore, I have used Paul's voice in every page. I have added some updated terms and references, but whenever I have done so, I've tried to set them off from the main text.

As I thought deeply about connecting with God, I was filled with a new sense of wonder. Down deep, we all long for connection. The enduring theme of this book is that it's possible for any of us to know God personally—to make the magnificent connection with God, through Jesus Christ. My prayer is that knowing *Whom* it is you believe in will be firmly secured in your life as well.

Marie H. Little

# FOREWORD

God has brought me in touch with certain men of outstanding talent. One such was my friend the late Paul Little, whom I first came to appreciate in a special way in 1957 when he tirelessly reached out to university students in our sixteen-week New York Crusade. I have deeply admired him as a man of God with extraordinary insights into the work of God and boundless enthusiasm for communicating the Word of God.

It was a great personal loss for me when Paul left us, and I feel privileged to recommend this stimulating series of talks, which he gave at The Village Church I once pastored in suburban Chicago.

In his unique way Paul describes "the electricity of Christ's claim," that He is the solution to the "moral power failure" of our time. Then he shows how Jesus Christ speaks to us today as clearly as He did to the thief on the cross: "You, too, can be with me in Paradise."

Maybe you have stood on the perimeter of Christianity and questioned what it is all about. *Is it really true? Does it have any pertinence to my life? What happens if I ignore it?* Or perhaps you have been discouraged in the past by some ponderous, cliché-ridden explanations. This book, then, is for you. You will find here an authenticity that comes from a man who was unconditionally devoted to Jesus Christ.

Billy Graham

# PART ONE

# Eight Bottom-Line Truths

# INNER DIRECTION NEEDED

*Does a Car Need a Driver?*

*A*sk *any ten people*
*what makes a person a Christian and*
*you'll get ten different answers.*

These words came out of my mouth unexpectedly at a dinner table where a group of friends, old and new, were relaxing over a third cup of coffee. The air was filled with lively conversation on an array of subjects. My wife and I knew the hosts well, but the others were new to us. Unexpectedly, one of the guests turned to me and asked what I was writing on. At that moment all I could think of to describe the ideas for this book was the above statement: "Ask any ten people what makes a person a Christian and you'll get ten different answers."

My new friend nodded his head with genuine sincerity, saying, "I'd be interested in having it boiled down for my thinking, too." As we talked, this gentleman soberly posed some stimulating questions about God and faith and how we acquire these ideas. We met again later and it was evident he was starting on a quest to sort out the true from the false.

Without overdoing it, here is a sampling of definitions I've heard in fraternities, university halls, and other places as I've traveled with

InterVarsity Christian Fellowship. Some ideas may have a grain of truth; others give a far-from-accurate picture.

I've heard a Christian is:

a. A Gentile: anyone not Jewish or an adherent of one of the world's major religions.

*Would an atheist like Madeleine Murray O'Hare want to be called a Christian?*

b. Someone who was born and raised in a Christian home or country, or who inherited their faith.

*Can faith be passed on through childbirth?*

c. A person who goes to church.

*Does going into a garage make you a car?*

d. Someone who practices rituals such as baptism, Communion, or Bible-reading.

*These activities may have value, but is the all-wise, personal God in the picture?*

e. One who follows the Golden Rule, and leads a moral life.

*Many good, moral people try to live by the Golden Rule yet make no claim to be Christians. Does merely following the teachings of Jesus give us a one-on-one connection with Him?*

f. A person who abstains from specific external, so-called "worldly" practices.

*A long list of "don'ts" or prohibitions might be seen as characteristic of some Christians. How does an emphasis on negatives fit in with Jesus Christ's message: "I have come that they may have life, and have it to the full" (John 10:10).*

g. Someone who gives casual intellectual assent to a certain list of beliefs.

*This could be a casual assent to the idea of God and Jesus Christ, like saying, "Oh yes, I believe all that I heard in church." Is belief a tentative list of ideas without a personal interchange or connection between the individual and God?*

Other ideas may come to our minds, but they further emphasize the importance of providing a clear answer to our beginning question: What makes a person a Christian? Some time ago I gave a talk at Queens University in Kingston, Ontario, on the reasonableness of Christianity. At the end, I opened the floor for discussion. A heavily bearded graduate student stood up, took his pipe out of his mouth, and asked, "Why do you Christians bother?" His underlying complaint of irrelevance went far beyond his words.

I was riveted by the young man's honesty. Christians "bother" because truth is at stake. None of the definitions above gives the full picture of the Christian message. Our understanding of the truth determines what we believe and trust. Coming to know the truth could be like the difference between being in a dark room and suddenly finding a light. It does matter what we think of God and Jesus Christ.

To illumine our thinking, these pages will lay out the bottom-line truths on which the Christian faith rests. The focus will be on the basics. What defines an authentic, inside Christian—not a superficial, casual type? We'll avoid discussing liturgical differences or minor doctrinal spin-offs and concentrate instead on the essentials, using the Bible as our truth source. We will find that the Bible spells out the extraordinary impact of Jesus' life, teaching, and identity. Who He was will naturally be the hub of this "Christian story."

## WE NEED DIRECTION

Our first bottom-line truth is "Inner Direction Needed." Jesus Himself advanced this idea to a group of highly religious people of His day. He saw the lives of some well-meaning people entirely absorbed with ceremonial rules and practices. They had strict procedures for washing their hands, the proper utensils to use, the kind of food to eat, and other endless rituals. Jesus told them: "Nothing that enters a man from the outside can defile him, since it enters not his heart but his stomach, and so passes on" (Mark 7:18). He went on to say it's what comes out of our hearts that matters. Who we are on the inside was of utmost importance to Him. I think you will agree it is to us, also.

It is interesting to note that Jesus discussed thoughts and actions in almost the same breath. For instance, He spoke of hatred and murder as equally culpable. He told people it is the inner heart that senses a need for help and poses the questions. Poet John Donne echoed that thought:

How little of a man is his heart
Yet it is all by which man is.[1]

Who of us hasn't had inner churning, wishing someone would listen to us, or even wondered if there anyone we can trust. *Are my friends and family trustworthy? What do ideas about God and Jesus Christ have to do with me in my everyday life? Does it matter what choices I make, what friends I hang out with, or what career I follow? Can I personally connect with God and Jesus Christ for certain in my inner self?* Some of us may have gone to a church or looked at the Bible hoping for answers.

In his song "Is Anybody There?" singer John Hiatt tells us of his inner feelings and at the same time strikes a chord of truth:

Well, I'm out here on my own
Followin' a star
Asking on my knees, for some direction, please
And, God, You know that's hard.[2]

In his heart Hiatt knew he needed help. Life was not going the way he felt it should, and something inside drove him to turn to God for an answer. If God doesn't care, who does? Hiatt got down on his knees and spoke to God through Jesus Christ. He poured out his heart. He sought Someone outside himself to bring relief. Someone BIG!

Such petitions germinate from the inner soul. St. Augustine described our "God-shaped vacuum that only God can fill." Asking questions defines us as humans; it's the natural thing to do. We feel we need help from someone outside of ourselves, but too often, seeking God and praying become our last and feeblest resort.

**God's love is more than you think.**

Let me assure you, there is hope. Throughout the Bible we see our Creator God directing, guiding, encouraging the people He created. He intended us to be in close relationship with Him—and this, in turn, affects our relationship with others. From the beginning pages of the Bible, God reached out to the people He created. He desired a "family" relationship. At one point in the story of the first couple, God Himself called to them, "Where are you?" (Gen. 3:9). God didn't want to be separated. Likewise, He calls to every one of us whom He created. "Come to me, and I will give you rest … " (Matt. 11:28)

10

### DOES A CAR NEED A DRIVER?

Imagine for a moment you are going into a car dealership and checking out a new car. The technical brilliance and the shining exterior of a new car are hard to resist. The latest model blows your mind with all the add-ons. But this enticing new machine has one unalterable deficiency. It will function only if it has an intelligent driver behind the wheel. Without a driver, an automobile is a mere museum piece. If you shoved one of these cars down a steep hill without a driver, it would careen and reel downward, wreaking damage along the way, and finally crashing.

Similarly, we human beings were made to be directed and led in life's path in close connection with our Maker. We function best when we get our cues from God. Unfortunately, each of us has individually shoved God out of the driver's seat of our lives. We continue to ratify this decision and handle our lives without reference to God. From early childhood, the knee-jerk reaction we follow is "I'll do it myself." We live our lives with this same kind of independence. "Don't drive me, God, I'll drive myself!"

Trying to live life without God, our incredibly wise Creator, is really as silly as being upset because we are dependent on air to breathe—and then holding our breath in rebellion! Cutting ourselves off from the one available Source of divine, nurturing power is like a tree cutting off its roots.

A car does need a driver; a tree does need roots; we do need air!

Author E. Stanley Jones quoted Carl Gustav Jung, famous European psychiatrist, as unexpectedly agreeing that we all need God:

"Those psychiatrists who are not superficial have come to the conclusion that the vast neurotic misery of the world could be termed a neurosis of emptiness. Men cut themselves from the root of their being, from God, and then life turns empty, inane, meaningless, without purpose, so when God goes, goal goes, when goal goes, meaning goes, when meaning goes, value goes, and life turns dead in our hands."[3]

We do need God! When God, "the root of our being," takes the wheel of our car, starts the engine, revs the motor, steers it in the right direction, and feeds us the right amount of fuel, life does *not* turn dead in our hands. Whatever our previous conceptions of God may be, our Creator's true, revealed purpose is to guide us onto the best road and in the wisest direction. Jeremiah describes it like this:

"This is what the LORD says, he who made the earth, the LORD who formed it and established it—the LORD is his name: Call to me and I will answer you and tell you great and unsearchable things you do not know" (Jer. 33:2-3).

To such an everlasting love, our best answer must be to tell Him with open hearts, "I need Your divine direction, Lord God." The call from God today has not changed. To each of us He says, "Where are you?" He initiates the call. He is interested in the details of our lives. Even in minor things He offers help to fill the "hole in our souls." This is the magnificent connection—you can actually know personally the God in whom you believe!

"My Presence will go with you, and I will give you rest" (Ex. 33:14).

"I have loved you with an everlasting love; I have drawn you with loving-kindness" (Jer. 31:3).

11

One young student, a Generation Xer, wrote openly of his final recognition of need and his honest cry for help: "Now—here is my secret: I tell it to you with an openness of heart that I doubt I shall ever achieve again, so I pray that you are in a quiet room as you hear these words. My secret is that I need God—that I am sick and can no longer make it alone. I need God to help me give, because I no longer seem to be capable of giving; to help me be kind, as I no longer seem capable of kindness; to help me love, as I seem beyond being able to love." [4]

(Douglas Coupland, *Life After God*, 1994)

## WHAT IS GOD LIKE?

If praying (talking to God) is new to us, we would naturally want to *know who* God is. Apart from definition, "God" means little to any of us. Without a clear description, our alternative would be a God of our own construction or imagination. There are a lot of wild guesses being sold in our bookstores and newspapers today. Some say God is an impersonal force, a ball of fire, and we are the sparks. Others see God as a celestial Santa Claus. We don't need idle guesses. We need certainty. Let's start with some tested and tried basics.

### God Is a Person

We can talk to Him. God is not a ghost or a puff of smoke. He has personality, mind, heart, and Spirit. As human beings, He created us in His image with individual personality, mind, heart, and spirit. Our all-powerful Creator is alive and approachable and is waiting for us to call on Him. He says:

"The Lord will guide you always" (Isa. 58:11).

"Come to me … for I am gentle and humble in heart, and you will find rest for your souls" are the words of Jesus (Matt. 11:28).

### God Reveals Himself

He has chosen to show Himself to us in a number of ways. We call this His "self-revelation." Most obviously, God can be seen as a superb artist in the magnificence of our created world and the complexity of our physical bodies. In everyday minor areas, I am thankful when my contact lenses feel dry that God created eyelids to blink and moisten them. I also marvel at the structure of my thumb and four fingers, telling me Someone ingenious designed them.

> **"God shows Himself not only in the Bible ... but also in the trees, flowers, clouds, stars."**
>
> *Martin Luther*

God revealed Himself specifically to the biblical writers and told them what to write. He used their individual personalities and their skills as poets or authors, and they recorded God's thoughts. He directed their entire lives. He told them He had plans for their lives, "plans to prosper you and not to harm you, plans to give you hope and a future" (Jer. 29:11). He unveiled His character and His will for them; He told them how to live productively. The entire message of the Bible, our source book, gives numerous details of God's regularly interacting with people. He sought them out, spoke to them directly, taught them, comforted them, and brought light to their lives. He gave national help and intervened in governments.

God directed individuals. He brought Elijah to full-blown victory when enemies challenged the nation's faith in God. He gave Job strong fortitude and deep spiritual insights when trouble hit him. In the New Testament, God spoke to a Christian named Ananias and told him to go to a Hebrew-trained man named Saul, who was praying. This Saul was transformed into the vibrant apostle Paul (Acts 9:11).

Then, supremely, we see God's love expressed in His sending His Son, Jesus Christ, to earth to communicate to us. In this act, He gave the fullest expression of His love. The eternal God reaches out to us, showing His desire to keep a close connection between Him and us. "This is how God showed his love among us: He sent his one and only Son into the world that we might live through him" (1 John 4:9). Isaiah gives a moving expression of God's initiative and care for His people (63:9).

In all their distress he too was distressed,
and the angel of his presence saved them.

13

> In his love and mercy he redeemed them;
>> he lifted them up and carried them all the days of old.

### God Is Love

He loves each of us personally. Motivated by love, He reaches out for a connection with us; He values what we do with our lives. Jesus tells us God numbers the hairs of our head and cares for our deepest needs. The Bible also tells us His love endures forever. He will not leave us when we face temptation, but His love draws us irresistibly to Himself. And most eloquently, "His steadfast love never ceases, His mercies never come to an end; they are new every morning" (Lam. 3:22, 23).

God's love is not expressed merely in propositional terms. His love is shown unmistakably in His actions. The Old Testament weaves persistent covenants and protection for all who would call on Him. The New Testament recounts detailed fulfillment of God's promises and actions in sending Jesus Christ, His Son. "For God so loved the world that he gave his one and only Son," Jesus Christ (John 3:16). This was love that *gave*. Here is a brief sample of the many pictures of God's love in action.

**God is not about to short-change us in life.**

Through the Son, God made the universe.

The Son is the radiance of God's glory.

He is the exact representation of God's being.

He sustains all things by His powerful word (Heb. 1:2, 3).

He is the One and Only, who has made God known (John 1:18).

"God's love is stronger than fire and destruction, and even in the valleys of deepest darkness, His rod and staff are put into our hands and bridges are thrown across the abyss." This was the moving declaration of German theologian Helmut Thielicke.[5]

### God Is Holy

God's nature is inherently without flaw. His instructions—His laws—are for our benefit, solely for our good.

It is not easy to fully comprehend God's holiness. Our world is shattered by senseless and vicious acts of evil that defy explanation. "God, why?" we ask. A simple answer is that God has given each of us the dignity of choice: choose to follow His path or choose evil and defy the Lord who made us.

Our own standards tell us to judge and punish mass murderers and terrorists and to feel justified in it. The little white lies or cheating on taxes we might forgive and feel no guilt about them. But down deep we know little sins become big ones and a second lie is often needed to cover up a first lie. Before we know it, lying becomes a habit. All of us want the other person to be honest. The fact is, Jesus said, all of us need to learn God's standard of holiness and we need forgiveness. *Any* sin separates us from our holy God. And His holiness is for our benefit.

Children feel hurt if we see them playing with a box of colored pushpins and we take the pins away. Is that fair? The child might wail and object, but you know it's right. Your desire is to protect the child. Likewise, God could not have slide-rule holiness. He knows where to draw the line. A student at the University of Kansas spoke to me after a lecture I'd given. Somewhat cavalierly he said, "If God grades on the curve, I'll make it." He had not yet comprehended God's unrivaled character. God doesn't grade on the curve!

God's standard is logical. Would God's presence and practice in heaven allow us to vote on our preference: shall we allow white lies or not? Imagine for a moment if God would allow even little lies into His presence in heaven. It would be certain to cause arguments, don't you think? God is 100 percent perfect. By definition He is completely without evil in thought, word, or deed. We may be better than someone else, but the other person is not our yardstick.

God's holiness is far above ours—total, unflawed goodness, a fixed incompatibility with inner or outer evil. Truthfully, when we understand His character, *His holiness is a comfort.* Anything less than perfection would not be God; it would be an imperfect human.

"I never knew God was an option in my life." This was the summary of a young man who had finally realized he needed to find out about God. He began his search with a determination to comprehend and act on the basics. We met in a large church meeting, struck up a friendship, and divulged our life stories to each other. In the end, the above potent phrase capsulized Bob's story. Of all his options in life, God never entered his mind. Would God—or could God—make a difference? He found the answer at a time when life was feeling like a tough ride.

On the surface, Bob seemed like a "together," archetypal man of the new millennium—educated and carefully groomed. He stood out as intentionally polite. Growing up in a financially well-heeled home, he believed appearances and wealth headed the list of necessities. His exterior made this evident. Underneath, his story revealed rougher waters. His father was rarely civil to him, and his mother lived on the opposite coast.

Although he looked like a highly cultured person, Bob repeated over and over his evil habits: his covert stealing at work, his passion for gambling, his expertise at lying—all lifelong habits, he confessed with an inconsolable sadness. He ended by talking about his two failed marriages, brought on by his own stinging hardness. When I asked if he had ever prayed to God or talked to a counselor, he replied, "When have I *not* been in counseling?"

Bob and I went to a small Bible study group together, and he seemed to be making valiant strides in attentively studying the life of Jesus Christ and the character of God. On and off I saw him, sometimes studying and regularly looking sad. Bob was known for a large-sized scrapbook he carried and in which he was determined to record the long list of regrettable habits of the past. One day he asked me to read his book with the remark, "These are things that I know God wants to change in my life. What should I do with them?"

"First of all, pray to God, in Jesus' name, tell Him you need His help to lead your entire life. Then, one by one, talk to Him about each of the habits you've struggled with. Ask Him for forgiveness. He'll tell you what to do," I told him. "God will also give you the power back-up that you need to follow Him, to go His way." I could see the wheels of his brain churning, but with a look of hope.

Almost six weeks passed before we had time to talk again. This time he said, "It's been hard. I haven't been certain I wanted Jesus to have my whole life, but now I'm ready. I want my entire life to be led by Him." Then he handed me his fabled book and asked if I would read it while he went to get us some coffee. When Bob returned, he told me he wanted to try to pray. "Take that book and burn it. It's all behind me," he said. We both prayed—Bob haltingly, but unmistakably sincere. I'll never forget his words to me as we parted: "Tell everyone about Jesus Christ, God's Son. He's the best option of all!"

This unforgettable line sums up one person's story of life change. Where we are in our journey matters to God. He is calling to each one of us, "Where are you?" We will find His open arms and unparalleled love waiting for us.

The next seven chapters will round out the eight bottom-line truths to make the magnificent connection and truly know personally the one in whom you believe—God. There is no greater relationship for any of us. And as G. K. Chesterton said: "Joy is the gigantic secret of the Christian."

## WRAP-UP #1: INNER DIRECTION NEEDED

1. Jesus' words: "It's what's inside, in the heart, that matters."

On a scale of 1-5, rate yourself. With reference to God, do you tend to emphasize external conduct or internal relationship? Circle.

1     2     3     4     5

2. From the chapter, describe some reasons you've learned for believing that "God's holiness is a comfort."

3. Considering that God is waiting for us with open arms and unparalleled love, which of these statements best describes where you are?

a. I have already given God the wheel and He is driving my life's car.

b. I would like to come forward and ask God for His direction.

17

*You will seek me and find me when you seek me*
*with all your heart.*
—Jer. 29:13

# JESUS CHRIST, THE CENTERPIECE

*The Divine shepherd has infinite attention
to spare for each one of us ... even a lost sheep.*
C. S. Lewis

Some years ago our family lived and worked in Switzerland with a Billy Graham Association Congress. An unexpected perk was that we were able to travel to places we had only read about in books. From the plethora of historic spotlights, I shall never forget our visit to the renowned Sistine Chapel in Rome with its acclaimed frescoes.

As we walked into the sizable chapel, largely devoid of furniture, a feeling of astonishment came over us. Every inch of the ceiling and walls was covered with breathtaking art. A number of other sightseers were standing transfixed around the room as they studied the frescoed walls. The ceiling, of course, was the centerpiece, with a single scene covering its entire length. Michelangelo spent four years suspended on a rack sixty-five feet above the floor, blending finely ground pigments and pasting them onto the damp plaster ceiling. Without doubt, the enticing message of this piece of art was apparent. The hand of God was pictured straining and stretching to clasp the hand of a man. Correspondingly, a man's hand was shown struggling to join his hand with God's, but it doesn't quite make it.

Both God and the man are revealing their built-in yearning to *connect*—hand to hand, skin to skin, Spirit to spirit—with the other. With uncanny brilliance, this fresco tells God and humanity's story from the beginning of Creation. Unlike any other relationship, God and man connecting is core of the Christian message.

The coming of Jesus Christ is the centerpiece of God and man's story. He was the One and Only, who came from the Father, full of grace and truth (John 1:14). In three years of public ministry Jesus repeated His message, calling people to come, follow Him. Twelve men left all and became His disciples full-time. Their lives were transformed. He demonstrated what a trusting relationship with Him would be like. He called to all the crowds who heard Him, "Come, follow Me." The apostle Peter testified, "Who else could we go to? You alone have the words of eternal life" (John 6:68).

Frequently Jesus used the words "I am" to underline His life's purpose and His identity. Six of these "I am" statements lay out the mind-stretching benefits for us when we connect with Him. They can help us see His compassion and the everyday practicality of a connection with the God who came to earth. We can be joined with Him hand to hand.

## UNCONDITIONAL LOVE AND COMPANIONSHIP

"I am the Good Shepherd: I know my own sheep and my own sheep know me" (John 10:14). A divine Shepherd for us! Jesus knows we need love and companionship, someone involved in our lives who prudently guides us as a shepherd guides his sheep. (In our day, we may not have observed sheep in action!) Every facet of a sheep's life is important to a shepherd. As a true friend knows the worst about us but still remains our friend, this is consummately true of Jesus as Shepherd. He knows we aren't prize packages, but He still loves us. He knows us better than we know ourselves. Connection with Him gives us love and companionship unequaled in human relationships.

Most of us think of shepherding as the equivalent of an earthly personnel manager who handles fifty or more people. The World Almanac says the 2002 world population is 6.157 billion people! Can even God handle that many people, let alone care for each one's microscopic problems? The answer is yes! Unquestionably, it is a divine Shepherd that is needed. We are talking about God Himself, our Creator. Jesus reached out to children, the needy, the intellectual, the wayward.

As our Shepherd, Jesus does not hand out lists of rules to obey but rather invites us to live close to Him. It is ironic that in this age of the greatest population explosion the world has ever known, more people are desperately lonely. For one thing, we are a rootless, mobile society in which people often don't live and die near relatives or have their support. There is suburban loneliness and urban loneliness. The highrise apartments we see in urban neighborhoods are monuments to loneliness. More than one person goes to the large shopping centers simply for the opportunity to talk to somebody in the stores, if only the supermarket checker.

> **"Jesus came from the Father, like a light from a lamp, heat from a fire, and thoughts from a mind."**
>
> C. S. Lewis

But there is a love without limit extended to each of us, whoever we are and wherever we are. Jesus' own parable tells the story we call "The Lost Sheep."

"Suppose one of you had a hundred sheep and lost one. Wouldn't you leave the ninety-nine in the wilderness and go after the lost one until you found it? When found, you can be sure you would put it across your shoulders, rejoicing, and when you got home call in your friends and neighbors, saying, 'Celebrate with me! I've found my lost sheep!' Count on it—there's more joy in Heaven over one sinner's rescued life than over ninety-nine good people in no need of rescue." (Luke 15:3-7, *The Message*)

When we feel no one cares about us and wonder if God is alive, we can recall Jesus' words about the one stray sheep. We will get God's view of us and the things we care about. The Shepherd left ninety-nine sheep to find and rescue one small lost one. It was urgent that this sheep be found and brought back to the fold and safety. The result was exultant joy in heaven because the lost one was found. The Shepherd, Jesus, is good. Relationship with Him can only be for our benefit. If a "thief or robber" attacks the sheep (John 10:8), He gives protection. He stands with us when evil and temptation pummel us, directs our thoughts, and guides our actions. Our part is to choose to follow His wise directions. A prescribed antibiotic tablet will zero in on a harmful bacterial infection and destroy it, but we must choose to swallow it. In a similar

21

way, when difficulty of any kind hits us, we find help when we turn to our Shepherd. "I know my sheep and my sheep know me. ... I lay down my life for the sheep" (John 10:14, 15).

A physician friend of mine had lived an unbridled immoral life obvious to all who knew him. One of his colleagues coaxed him into going to a lecture for the Christian Medical Society. At the lecture, he told me, for the first time, he saw there was a way out for him that drew him to consider giving his life to Jesus Christ. He told me he felt all alone and it was not pleasant. That night he made a commitment to Christ, and when we parted, I was cheered to see his confident stride and an upbeat expression on his face.

About a year after this commitment, some of his longtime colleagues asked him, "When you're away from all your religious friends and by yourself, don't you sometimes miss your old friends and wish you could get back into the old life with us?" The doctor looked at them and said, "Yes, sometimes I do, but then I realize that I am never alone. Now I know Jesus Christ is with me, and I've found He helps me over the rough spots."

## THE WHERE, WHAT, AND HOW OF OUR LIVES

"I am the light of the world." Jesus made this statement immediately after an encounter with a lonely, troubled woman (John 8:1-11). She was surrounded by a group of religious leaders who were pointing accusing fingers at her. She had sinned—was caught in the very act of adultery—and now she would have to pay for it. The leaders were hoping to trap Jesus and test Him. Would He obey their tradition, which allowed them to stone her? What would He do? Jesus knew the hearts of these accusers. Without flinching, He said, "If any one of you is without sin, let him be the first to throw a stone at her." Convicted, these men paused, watched His demeanor as He wrote in the sand, and gradually, one by one, the accusers left.

"Who is accusing you?" Jesus asked her.

"No one."

"Nor do I condemn you," He said, and added, "Go, and leave your life of sin."

In this brief encounter and few words with the woman, Jesus brought more light to her than she probably had ever known. He could have sided with the accusers, treated her roughly, derided her actions. But He was controlled and thoughtful. His light came with compassion. He wanted to forgive the woman and get her going in the right direction. He defended her even though she had made some wrong turns in her life. He told the truth: she had sinned. She had harmed herself and other people and disobeyed God. Then He gave her hope that a change could take place. "Go, leave your sin."

It was after this that Jesus turned to the disciples who were with Him and said, "I am the light of the world, he who follows me will not walk in darkness, but will have the light of life" (John 8:12).

His light brings us His understanding of our weaknesses and gives us His wise solutions. Here are a few specific areas of how He shows us light.

• First, Jesus' light tells us *where* we originated. We were created by the God of the universe, each person so unique that even our individual human genome is unduplicated by anyone else's. As His unique creation, we have intrinsic value.

• Second, Jesus' light shows us *what* is the best purpose for life, the best choices for the small things and the large. When we view each day as having eternal purpose, honoring Him and following His pattern of serving others, it gives a different slant to our days. "What would Jesus do?" is a good question and leads us in a path that will honor Him. Each of us has a valuable slot and notch no one else can fill.

Even the routine chores of life such as mowing the lawn, changing the diapers, guiding our families, washing the dishes, studying physics, and playing chess tie in with His purpose as surely as the so-called spiritual aspects of our lives such as praying, going to church or reading the Bible. Every part of life is meaningful when we see it through His eyes and as a service to Him.

• Third, Jesus' light tells us *how* to live. His kind of life is without masks, nothing to hide and motivated by the kind of love He shows. Like the circle of light drawn by a flashlight in a dark woods, His light draws safe parameters for us, a circumference of values to keep us from stumbling. "His word is a lamp to our feet" (Ps. 119: 105).

Have you have ever tried to love someone who appears chronically unlovely? You know it is not possible by pumping yourself up and saying, "I ought to love them, I ought to love them. I will think positively about them and begin to love." It is possible, however, if we turn to Jesus Christ and ask Him to give us His view of the person. Looking at people through Jesus' eyes, He makes the impossible possible.

Our lives may feel dark, our will to face another day can be small, but His light will restore our perspective. Let us plug into the power source, and we will find ourselves smiling instead of grumbling. When light comes, darkness, of necessity, leaves. The two cannot exist together.

The apostle Paul said, "We have the mind of Christ" (1 Cor. 2:16). After Paul met Jesus Christ, he literally turned the world upside down. Jesus Christ, the light, will also show each of us the where, what, and how for our lives.

## SPIRITUAL FULFILLMENT

"I am the bread of life" (John 6:48). Recognition of the need for inner fulfillment beyond the material came from surprising quarters. Some years ago, a novel entitled *Not by Bread Alone* was smuggled out of the former Soviet Union. The author verified the reports of a society dedicated to the philosophic proposition that only the material is real. Even in this environment many held on to their Christian faith. They reached for something beyond the material.[6] The title of the above book came from Jesus' words: "I am the bread of life; he who comes to me shall never hunger, and he who believes in me shall never thirst" (John 6:35).

> **The Centerpiece is God Incarnate, not your ordinary mystic guru.**

When the stomach is empty, it calls for food. When the spirit is empty, our feelings smolder, sometimes grow bitter, and even a best friend may be unable to console us. We might seek other palliatives, but the place inside calls for spiritual bread, that is, contentment and peace from our divine Creator. To this inner space inside us Jesus promises to be our bread of life, our sustenance, our filling, our satisfaction, in circumstances good or bad.

The apostle Paul was imprisoned, beaten, and thrown out of cities, but he was strengthened because he was nourished by the true "bread of life." He said, "I have learned to be content whatever the circumstances" (Phil. 4:11). Paul didn't appreciate prisons and scorpions and snakes and rats any more than we do, but he had something deep inside that sustained him. Early Christians actually went singing into dens of lions fortified by the inner sustenance Jesus gave them.

A beginning Christian read some of the chapters of this manuscript and stopped at this section on the bread of life. He heavily underlined Jesus' words declaring that He is the bread of life. In the margin the young man wrote, "Be sure to underline this. I needed Jesus' bread for a long time before I found Him."

## POWER OVER MORAL FAILURE

"I am ... the life" (John 14:6). Guilt or immorality needs more than good advice, more than new rules. Jesus Christ knew that if all He did when He came into human history was to give us the Sermon on the Mount or underline the Ten Commandments, as great as they are, He would have only increased our frustrations. There has been some form of the Golden Rule from at least the time of Confucius.

Jesus saw the need for a different tack altogether; He saw that big sins or little sins require divine help. His coming to earth was for the sole purpose of giving new life—His life, God coming beside us to help. He is not like a person standing on the shore of a river who sees a man drowning and throws him a set of swimming instructions to read. He came to earth and dove into the waters of our world—polluted beyond belief—to tell us He wants to give us help. "I am *the* life," He said.

Jesus' supernatural life and power give us:

• Release from entrenched destructive habits
• Awareness of evil
• God's supernatural power to overcome temptation

His power is strong enough to make a liar tell the truth, to make a prostitute pure, to make a thief honest. His power can break the chain of drug addiction, the prison of alcoholism, the deceit of self-centeredness, the pride of criticism. Jesus described His coming to us as new life, new birth, a new person inside. This is supernatural help.

Unconsciously our postmodern worldview and mores are absorbed and accepted without question. From TV, the print media, music, mystics, pop authors, and peers, we follow (sometimes like robots) the material world. Trustworthy light is our safest route.

## FORGIVENESS AND FREEDOM

"The Son sets you free" (John 8:36). Jesus spelled out this message to some ordinary people of His day. He knew their inner needs and said simply, "everyone who sins is a slave to sin" (vs. 34). Not one of us is without some hidden inner shortfall. These may be external, blatant wrongdoing or secret, silent thoughts. We can become addicted, caught in the grip of a habit, unable to change, stuck. This includes all of us. The place to start, He said, is to ask for forgiveness for past sins. "So if the Son [Himself] sets you free, you will be free indeed" (John 8:36).

"I was so corrupt that I needed a bath!" I heard this man's story of desperation at a university student meeting. He told us it was a year before he gave his life to Jesus Christ through the ministry of Dr. Fred

The subtlety of moral drift hit us unawares with the flood of accolades over a book and film, *The Bridges of Madison County*. From the reviews, I learned the story line apparently totally overlooked the possibility of marital fidelity. One lonely reviewer in the *Chicago Tribune* opined, "How noble a movie it would have been had its writers shown the Iowa farm wife, in her moment of weakness, held resolutely to her marital promise." Instead, she concluded her affair made her "more like myself than ever before." Her daughter followed suit and threw over her own marriage. The promise "Till death do us part" never entered the picture.[7]

I read the above review to a young friend of mine, who thanked me for pointing it out to him. Although a Christian for a long period of time, he had completely missed the lack of fidelity in the movie as the skill of Clint Eastwood and Meryl Streep enthralled him. He thanked me because he had forgotten to evaluate the content implicit in the film in the light of his Shepherd's values, and he wanted to develop a discerning mind.

Marie Little

26

Smith, a professor at the University of Minnesota. The man said, "My life was so racked up that I didn't know which way to turn. The corruption on my inside was so bad that I needed a bath from the inside out. When I came to know Jesus Christ, I got that bath. I can't describe the difference that came over me. For twenty-four hours after this happened, I just sat, thinking about the implications and the penetrating force I experienced. I knew I was forgiven."

We have the choice to stay in our rut of moral ambivalence, tolerating no interference from God or anyone else. Or, like this man, we can respond to Jesus' offer of forgiveness.

The apostle Paul says it simply: "For he has rescued us from the dominion of darkness and brought us into the kingdom of the Son he loves, in whom we have redemption, the forgiveness of sins" (Col. 1:13, 14). He also says we have forgiveness of sins "in accordance with the riches of God's grace that he lavished on us" through Jesus Christ (Eph. 1:7, 8). His conclusion: forgiveness is a mystery that displays the extent of God's care for us.

## INNER PEACE

Some of the most eloquent and consoling words that Jesus Christ ever uttered show us His peace and rest.

"Peace I leave with you; my peace I give you. I do not give to you as the world gives. Do not let your hearts be troubled, and do not be afraid" (John 14:27).

"Come to me, all you who are weary and burdened, and I will give you rest" (Matt. 11:28).

*Rest* and *peace* are the kind of words we need to experience inwardly. We can munch on their meaning and truth as we would savor a favorite food. They comfort us when we turn our thoughts to the One who promised them and ask how they apply to our life situations. He said, "My peace I give to you." The eternal true God brings powerful, lasting peace.

A girl from Barnard College came to our home when we were living in New York. She unburdened a story of deep hurts— so deep she felt she couldn't trust her own family, let alone anyone else. We read together the exact prescription for her hurt, Jesus' words from John 14:18: "I will not leave you as orphans; I will come to you."

Winsomely, the young girl said with tears, "You mean to say He'll never leave me?" As we talked about our Shepherd, we were soon laughing easily at the awesome prospect of divine help.

Can you see, Jesus Christ is not just a good idea; He is a living person. His kind of life is not a mere modicum of help or a quick fix; it is overflowing, clear-eyed living and a relationship that lasts for a lifetime connected with the Divine Centerpiece. This is not your common, ordinary connection!

Connect with Jesus, the Centerpiece

| Shepherd | John 10:14 |
| Light | John 8:22 |
| Bread | John 6:35 |
| Life | John 14:6 |
| Freedom | John 8:36 |
| Peace | John 14:27 |

## WRAP-UP # 2: JESUS CHRIST, THE CENTERPIECE

1. From Jesus' six "I Am" statements, record what personal help each one could bring to your life:

    a. Shepherd

    b. Light

    c. Bread

    d. Life

    e. Freedom

    f. Peace

2. What ideas have been new to your mind from:

    a. God's deep desire to connect with you

    b. Jesus' extravagant offers to help you

# ALONE ON THE STAGE OF HISTORY

*The eternal God is made known
in the personality and life of His Son,
Jesus Christ.*

I stared at the Christmas card on my desk. From a background of red, bold white letters trumpeted a single phrase, "His birth split time in two." The words seized me; I could not forget them. One man's birth, over two thousand years ago, rocked the world. It changed its calendar and tailored its mores. The atheist in America dates his checks with 2003, declaring His birth. The rulers of countries in both East and West, regardless of their religions, use His birth date as well. Unthinkingly we declare His birth on letters, legal documents, and appointment books. On Christmas Day, memorializing His birth, the mall parking lots are starkly empty.

An unknown author penned this capsule description:

He was born in an obscure village.
He worked in a carpenter shop until He was thirty.
He then became an itinerant preacher.

He never held an office.
He never had a family or owned a house.
He didn't go to college.
He had no credentials but Himself.

Twenty centuries have come and gone,
and today He is the central figure of the human race.

All the armies that ever marched
and all the navies that ever sailed,
all the parliaments that ever sat
and all the kings that ever reigned

Have not affected the life of man
on this earth as much as this
*One solitary life.*

Who was this Jesus? How did His power and influence encompass the entire globe? In thirty-three short years, He impacted His own generation and more than two thousand years of generations that followed.

Not long ago, Michael, who was an above-average student, won a student exchange term abroad. He ended his study period and took the opportunity to cruise through as many European countries as he could with his limited funds.

As far as I knew, Michael was a Christian. He did all the right things at the right time. He seemed headed toward a successful career and the American good life. When I talked to him, I became aware he had something he urgently wanted to talk about. He began by giving a few cursory details about his itinerary and then spouted, "Amsterdam changed my life!"

"The city of Amsterdam?" I asked him, somewhat puzzled.

Michael began to describe in detail the parks, the central, bawdy part of the city, the waterfront, all dotted with people. Some neatly dressed, some unkempt, and others glassy-eyed. Many of them were young people. The world was different there, he told me. People appeared to be going nowhere, a lot of them moved in slow motion from one bar to another, hanging loosely on each other and at times poised ready to pick a fight.

At the end of his story, Michael shuddered as he said, "As I watched them, I saw that the only difference between those people and me was *Jesus Christ.*"

"I was very close to selling everything I had to get the next shot of drugs when I heard about Jesus. I prayed to Him and asked for His help, and before I knew it, I was packing to go home. He gave me the power that was outside myself to walk away from this magnetic force siphoning my entire existence!" It was hard for me to envision Michael as unkempt or glassy-eyed, but I knew that the power of commitment to Jesus Christ can radically change a person.

Michael's story of life change could be told by me and innumerable others—the rich, the poor, the unknown, the famous. The story is the same—it's the powerful impact of a man who lived over two thousand years ago. What was Jesus Christ, this incredible man, really like? Was He God come to earth, as He said? How has it happened that the Michaels of this world ended up worshiping Him?

## JESUS TOUCHED THE WHOLE GAMUT OF SOCIETY

Beginning at thirty years of age, Jesus preached continuously a mere three years. "The large crowd listened to him with delight," the writer Mark reported (Mark 12:37). Today, many of His words—the Beatitudes, the Golden Rule, the Prodigal Son—are a part of our everyday language.

**This man Jesus: was the *exact* representa-tion of God's glory.**

*Heb. 1:2, 3*

The common people were His constant companions; fishermen and political activists were among his twelve disciples. The morally outcast, the politically despised, the physically sick, and the racially shunned were touched by Him. Zacchaeus was an immoral, tax-cheating traitor whose lifestyle was turned 180 degrees after a single encounter with Jesus. The sick, the blind, the ordinary people numbering in the thousands listened to Jesus. Intellectual and religious leaders pondered His every word. A legalistic separatist, Nicodemus, queried Him under the cover of night to get his questions answered. A wealthy member of the Jewish high court named Joseph of Arimathea buried Him in his own tomb.

At His birth He was given the name Jesus, meaning "Savior," to express the special office He would fulfill: "he will save his people from their sins" (Matt. 1:21). His title is Christ, meaning "Anointed One," someone who is appointed to a special position or service. Peter declared, "You are the Christ, the Son of the living God"

(Matt. 16:16). The title Messiah carries the same meaning and is used in both the Old and New Testaments.

## Jesus Displayed Supernatural Power over Disease, Demons, and Death

A cursory listing of some of Jesus' miracles helps us see this was no ordinary man!

> At a wedding, Jesus turned water into wine.
>
> He fed over 5,000 people with only five loaves of bread and two fish. (After this, the people, understandably, wanted to make Him king!)
>
> He calmed a savage storm in which seasoned fishermen were fearful for their lives.
>
> He gave sight to a man who was blind from birth.
>
> He raised Lazarus from the dead.
>
> He healed a man torn to self-destruction by a demon.

## Jesus' Moral Character Was Impeccable

Skeptics and unbelievers alike have agreed that Jesus personified the pinnacle of ethical behavior. His moral life and character were demonstrably without flaw. He forthrightly asked His scheming religious critics, "Can any of you prove me guilty of sin?" (John 8:46). No one replied, for there was no condemning evidence against Him. In all of the written record of His life He did not confess His own sin, as was commonly practiced by other so-called saints.

His friends said:

> He did no sin, neither was guile found in his mouth (1 Pet. 2:22).
>
> He knew no sin (2 Cor. 5:21).
>
> In Christ there is no sin (1 John 3:5).

His enemies said:

> I find no fault in Him (Pilate, the acting Roman governor, Luke 23:4).
>
> This was an innocent man (Pilate's wife, Matt. 27:19).
>
> I have betrayed [Jesus'] innocent blood (Judas, Matt. 27:4).
>
> Surely he was the Son of God! (Roman centurion who watched Jesus crucified, Matt. 27:54).

**This man Jesus:** **He** *created* *everything* **in heaven and earth ...**

*Heb. 1:2, 3*

## Jesus Declared He Was God Come to Earth

Jesus made pointed statements regarding who He was. "I am the way, the truth and the life" (John 14:6). "I and the Father [God] are one" (John 10:30). "If you know me, you would know God" (John 8:19). "If you've seen me, you've seen the Father [God]" John 14:9. "Come to me and I will give you abundant life" (John 10:10).

To put this in perspective today, suppose I should say to you, "If you know me, you know God." Your response would doubtless be that I urgently needed some help. Certainly, you would not take me seriously.

**This man Jesus: He** *sustains* *all things* **by His power ...**

*Heb. 1:2, 3*

With Jesus, people took Him seriously. There were events and actions that anyone in the crowd could see that made His repeated claims believable and undeniable, even captivating. People left their work and businesses and dropped everything to follow Him.

## Jesus' Followers Eloquently Described Him as God

The writer of Hebrews says: "He reflects the glory of God and bears the very stamp of God's nature" (Heb. 1:3).

Paul says: "He is the image of the invisible God" (Col. 1:15).

Peter says: "God the Father ... has given us new birth through Jesus Christ" (1 Pet. 1:3).

John calls Him the "Word of life" (1 John 1:1).

Thomas says: "My Lord and my God," on seeing the scars in Jesus' hands proving that He was resurrected (John 20:28).

Indeed, through Him all things in heaven and on earth were created. He made the universe; He holds all things together. He is the exact representation of God's being, the radiance of God's glory (Col. 1:16; Heb. 1:2; Heb. 1:3).

## Jesus Fulfilled the Prophecies in the Old Testament

Hundreds of years before Jesus was born, many prophets in the Old Testament foretold His coming in specific detail. The New Testament writer Luke relates an unforgettable example of one of these prophecies. When Jesus first started teaching, in keeping with Jewish tradition, He went to the synagogue regularly.

One day in the synagogue at Nazareth where Jesus grew up, He stood to read to those gathered. A special attendant in charge of the parchment scrolls handed Him a scroll of the prophet Isaiah. Jesus unrolled the scroll and began to read the eight hundred-year-old document.

Jesus read Isaiah 61:1, 2.

"The Spirit of the Sovereign Lord is on me,

Because the Lord has anointed me

To preach *good news* to the poor,

To *bind up* the broken hearted,

To proclaim *freedom* to the captives

And *release from darkness* for the oppressed.

To proclaim the year of the Lord's favor (Luke 4:18, 19).

He then rolled up the scroll, handed it back to the attendant, and sat down. No one who heard Him moved; every eye in the place was fixed on Him, intent on His next action. He stood up, started deliberately, and made this unprecedented announcement: "Today, this Scripture is fulfilled in your hearing" (Luke 4:21).

Imagine the electricity of someone saying He fulfilled a prophecy written 800 years before! The expectancy of the listeners turned to wonder and fascination. "All were amazed at the gracious words that came from His lips," Luke described it (v. 22). No one challenged Him; they sat there waiting. Watching Him closely, they could see this was no ordinary man and the verses seemed to fit what they had seen of His life in the short time He had been teaching. There was power in His presence.

The watching crowd asked if this wasn't the hometown boy, the son of the carpenter Joseph. Next, they wanted Him to do miracles for them. Yet they felt a restraining reverence for Him when He read Isaiah.

In the thirty-three years Jesus lived, well over sixty specific prophecies were fulfilled from the Old Testament, giving meticulous details of His life impossible to refute. It would be similar to us today predicting a person would be born in the year 2802 A.D., plus where he would be born and what he would do. Most of the prophecies about Jesus were written seven hundred or more years before His birth. Naturally speaking, impossible.

The prophet Isaiah in the fifty-third chapter lists fifteen specific details of Jesus' death.Verses 3 to 12 speak of His suffering, rejected by His people, silent before His accusers, took our sins on Himself, treated unjustly, buried with rich people, and raised from the dead. It has been said the odds of just eight prophecies being fulfilled in exact detail in one person would be 1 in 10 to the 17th power—that is, one with 17 zeros after it. Ask your local math expert about that! The odds defy imagination.

Three detailed prophecies with their dates written and dates fulfilled are listed here.

| OLD TESTAMENT PROPHECY | NEW TESTAMENT FULFILLMENT |
|---|---|
| Born in Bethlehem Micah 5:2 700 B.C. | Jesus born in Bethlehem Matt. 2:1-6 4 B.C. |
| He was pierced for our transgressions, crushed for our iniquities. Isa. 53:5 800 B.C. | One of the soldiers pierced Jesus' side with a spear, bringing a sudden flow of blood and water. John 19:34 29 A.D. |
| They paid me thirty pieces of silver. . . . So I took the thirty pieces of silver and threw them into the house of the LORD to the potter. Zech. 11:12-13 500 B.C. | They counted out for him thirty silver coins. ... Judas threw the money into the temple. ... They decided to use the money to buy the potter's field. Matt. 26:15; 27:5, 7 29 A.D. |

35

Malcolm Muggeridge, in his book *Jesus, The Man Who Lives*, describes the biblical words of Jesus as "the inviolate genes of the Christian faith." Muggeridge continues:

"To the glory of these words Bach composed, El Greco painted, Augustine labored at his 'City of God', Bunyan found his inspiration in prison to write of a Pilgrim's journey through the wilderness of this world, and Sir Thomas More was comforted on his way to the scaffold."[8]

## GOOD NEWS IS FORGIVENESS

Jesus strode toward His goal to make good news and forgiveness possible for anyone who would trust Him. One day Jesus was teaching in a small house and a crowd jammed into the place to hear Him teach. The doors were blocked and the windows clogged with eager listeners. Four men carrying a paralyzed friend who hoped to be healed were unable to get past the crowd. These men climbed onto the roof, dug through the tiles above where Jesus stood, and lowered the man down through the hole.

Upon seeing the sick man and the faith of his friends, Jesus simply told the man his sins were forgiven! The religious experts were appalled, because they knew that only God could forgive sins. Unperturbed, Jesus told the sick man to get up, roll up his bed, and walk. Immediately, the man did! "He got up, took his mat and walked out in full view of them all"—a man paralyzed all his life! In so many words, Jesus said, "OK, now will you believe Me? I healed him because I wanted you to know that I have power to forgive sins as only God has." Deep inside they knew forgiving sins was God's territory, not man's.

Even the critics and the others praised God and said they had never seen anything like this before. Now, that's impact! You can read about it in Mark 2:1-12.

The primacy of helping the needy sometimes drew so-called disreputable characters to follow Jesus. In fact, Jesus' enemies called Him "a friend of tax collectors and 'sinners'" (Matt. 11:19). He was having dinner with such a group when the religious people lit into Jesus' followers: "What kind of example is this from your Teacher, acting cozy with the crooks and riffraff?"

Overhearing them, Jesus shot back, "Who needs a doctor: the healthy or the sick? . . . I am after mercy, not religion. I'm here to invite outsiders, not coddle insiders" (Matt. 9:12, *The Message*). Like a magnet, His compassion drew Him to hurting people—and they to Him. "Never a man spoke like this man" repeatedly described Him. The panorama of His life pictures for us God come to earth. He was both God and man, divine and human.

More than two millennia later, this man continues to connect with the lives of people, with those who will trust Him. His power has not diminished. In the future, there will come a day when all people will see Him, as theologian Helmut Thielicke projected it:

"When the final history of the world is told, the names of great and small are listed, many with superb records of great deeds and accomplishments, we will salute them. Many deserve our attribution.

"Towering over all, alone on the stage of history will stand One, not just a fine, good man, but the only One who is God incarnate; the exact representation of God in human form, begotten of God. The Deliverer and Savior."[9]

## WRAP-UP #3: ALONE ON THE STAGE OF HISTORY

1. We have looked at the solid evidence of God, the infinite, penetrating our finite world with Jesus' coming. Which Godlike characteristics were most convincing to you of Jesus' divinity? Note your impressions on the following points:

    a. His attitude to people

    b. His power over nature disease, demons, death

    c. His moral character

    d. His self-description as God

    e. His followers' eloquent descriptions

    f. Fulfilled prophecy

    g. His good news of forgiveness

37

*"The Word [Jesus] became flesh and made his dwelling
among us."*
—John 1:14

# LOVE AND JUSTICE MEET

*Good news! Jesus' death puts us
in good standing with God,
gives us a fresh start.*

If you were to visit a large church near our home, you might be struck with the fact, as a friend of ours was, that there is no cross evident anywhere. "A church without a cross?" he exclaimed. He knew the centrality of the cross to the Christian message. He also discovered that some churches display it more than others. Metallic crosses decorate spiral roofs, the interiors of churches, and jewelry counters. It is considered fashionable to wear a cross. But what is the true meaning of the cross of Jesus Christ?

The cross is good news. When we fully understand it, it can also be rightfully called God's magnificent design. On the surface, Jesus Christ dying an undeserved, cruel death on a cross seems flagrantly inappropriate, to say the least—bizarre, if nothing else. Unless, that is, we grasp two fixed truths:

    a. the extent of God's love that designed the cross

    b. our assured need for forgiveness

John Bunyan's allegory, *The Pilgrim's Progress*, gives us a picture of the power of the cross. A man named Christian started to wend his way through a chain of encounters desperately seeking the true way to the Celestial City (heaven). On his back he carried a hulking burden of trials, temptations, failures, doubts, immorality, yet he determined to find the correct way. He followed a variety of circuitous and dead-end routes, stumbling every step. At last he met someone who told him "the only Way" to be free was through the cross of Jesus Christ on the hill of Calvary.[10]

I read this story as a new Christian, and I can still visualize Christian in his arduous struggle up a steep hill to the top where the cross stood. His heart heavy, Christian finally arrived at the crest, knelt prostrate before the foot of the cross, and prayed for help. At last, to his great wonder, his heavy load fell off and rolled down the hill. The change was instant. He was freed from his burden of sins, forgiven for the first time in his life. He stood up, descended the hill with exhilaration, and continued his life's journey toward the Celestial City joyously singing this song:

"Blessed cross, blessed sepulcher,
Blessed rather be the Man
Who there was put to shame for me."

G. K. Chesterton described the hill on which Jesus was slain:
"Where life was slaughtered and truth was slain/
On that holier hill than Rome."[11]

## POWERFUL GOOD NEWS

The message of the cross, when understood, brings celebration and joy. It is God's Good News demonstrating His love for us. Whatever our past history of living without connection with God or concern for right and wrong, His care persists. Christian saw his heavy load of sin roll down the hill; his lifelong burden was gone. He had every reason to rejoice.

When we know we are forgiven, a sense of relief wells up within us. The old mistakes are forgiven; we can admit our failures and confess them, knowing He will free us. This message gives us strong evidence of God's enduring, eternal connection with us. The cross gives us this assurance. John the Baptist saw Jesus coming and shouted to the crowd, "Look, this is the One who comes to take away the sins of the world" (John 1:29). And the apostle John wrote, "This is love: not that we loved God, but that he loved us and sent his Son as an atoning sacrifice for our sins" (1 John 4:10).

God, our Creator, had firm reason behind His intentional design and planned it before He created the world. At least seven times in the New Testament the death of Christ is described as "planned before the world's creation" (Rev. 13:8). This was no last-minute decision on God's part to send His Son to the cross. No "Oops, man has strayed away. Now what do we do?" If we carefully study the entire "story of God" from the beginning of the Bible until Jesus' coming, we will see the theme of sacrifice and forgiveness that climaxed at the cross.

> **In God, love and Justice are perfectly balanced. He is 100% loving and 100% just.**

Jesus spoke frequently about His future destiny, not as a misunderstood martyr, but as a person with a goal and timetable. He mentioned it to His disciples a number of times with phrases like "My hour is not yet come," "I have come to give my life a ransom for many," and "I have come to seek and save the lost."

Jesus described His approaching death on the cross at the Last Supper the night before the Crucifixion. As He sat at the table with His twelve disciples, He told them He was going to die. Pointedly, He said the purpose of His death was to bring forgiveness: "Eat the bread and drink the wine to remember My death, for the forgiveness of sins" (Matt. 26:28). Not comprehending the full meaning of this, His disciples ate with Him, then they all left the room and went out into an olive garden. In the late-night hours they saw Jesus willingly allow Himself to be taken away by the band of angry Roman soldiers. "He humbled himself and became obedient to death—even death on a cross!" (Phil. 2:8).

## WHY COULDN'T GOD JUST FORGIVE US?

Why did Jesus have to die? A logical question to ask. Think for a moment: would abolishing all punishment solve the problem of evil either here in our world or in heaven with God? Should all laws of our government be canceled? The truth is, payment for committed sin is a given in a moral world.

For every crime, there is a cost, a price. If someone wrecks our car, someone must pay to have it fixed. If I spill gravy on a woman's expensive silk dress, either she or I must pay. Some payments are decided by human laws; some payments are decided by God's laws. Usually payments for wrongs are logical, based upon the destructiveness of the evil. It occurred to me that every religion in the world requires some retribution or cost for not following their laws and ways.

None of us would allow the Unabomber to continue his killing spree without some punishment. Nor can we excuse drunken drivers. Even traffic laws must exact penalties or consequences. Can we comprehend the antipathy of our perfect God to evil? His eyes are "too pure to look on evil" (Hab. 1:13). For the one eternal God, every sin-debt must be paid.

## LOVE AND JUSTICE MEET

The good news is that God's love and justice are perfectly balanced at the cross. With God, His moral character and wisdom would not allow it otherwise. He could not have two pounds of love and only one pound of justice, or vice versa.

Humanly speaking, we tend to wish for more love than justice from our Creator God. But He is not like a doting grandparent who can be manipulated to change His standards. (Thankfully, not all grandparents fit this image!) If God were overly loving and doting, fairness or justice would not be in the picture. Only love would be expressed regardless of circumstances. Personal responsibility for actions, or right and wrong, would not be considered.

Our culture and our thinking do not easily comprehend God's truth and righteousness. With God there can be no slide-rule standard. When TV host Larry King asked defense attorney Robert Shapiro if he was in pursuit of the truth in O. J. Simpson's case, Shapiro answered sharply, "Absolutely not." After that, he shrugged off any personal opinion or moral judgment about the truth or justice in this case. Thankfully, Shapiro is not God. God must be both loving and just!

There is no ambivalence in the biblical picture of God. He is 100 percent loving; He is 100 percent just. The word *just* is defined as "righteous, fair, equitable." Measured against His perfection, we all need forgiveness. We may be better than someone else, or worse than someone else, but heaven, by definition, can be no less than absolute perfection. Again, God's rightness and loving-kindness have designed a redemptive answer: the cross. His fairness and sinlessness are a comfort.

Some time ago there was the account of a commercial airliner that crashed into a mountaintop while trying to land at the Las Vegas airport in a snowstorm. The most tragic thing about the crash was that it occurred only a couple of feet from the top of the mountain. Another few feet and the plane would have made it over the mountaintop. Sadly, all of those people were as dead as if they had crashed a thousand feet farther down. In terms of the ultimate goal to get over the mountain, each one on the plane needed rescuing.

The ultimate objective of the airliner was to go higher than the top of the mountain. In a similar way, God's perfect standard of morality in heaven is far beyond our earthly ability to attain. We all "fall short of the glory of God," as Romans 3:23 puts it.

From the beginning of the Bible, God's solution for our moral deficit was the sacrificial system. Offerings of animals and grains were brought to the Lord in thanksgiving and celebration and as evidence of repentance for wrongdoing. The sacrifices offered to God brought forgiveness to the person who offered them. They were offered in place of the person who gave them. These Old Testament animal sacrifices clearly prefigured the sacrifice of Christ, as the psalmist and prophets predicted.

The extraordinary design of the cross displays one almighty God dying for all people everywhere. This is not a mere human dying to pay the debt for one other human being; it is the eternal God Himself offered as a sacrifice for every person born into the world. The sentence, the punishment that should have fallen on us, fell on Him. We are the beneficiaries of God's merciful design.

One person can take the punishment for another person.

One God can take the punishment for every person on the planet.

Two areas are covered by the sacrifice of Jesus Christ:

a. He took our punishment.

"The LORD has laid on him the iniquity of us all" (Isa. 53:6).

"He himself bore our sins in his body on the tree" (1 Pet. 2:24).

b. We become a "new creation."

"If anyone is in Christ he is a new creation; the old has gone, the new has come!" (2 Cor. 5:17).

"God made him who had no sin to be sin for us, so that in him we might become the righteousness of God" (2 Cor. 5:21).

Without a doubt, our best life choice is to admit our need and kneel at the cross of Christ, as John Bunyan's Christian did. Here God's love and justice are wedded in ideal symmetry.

## GRACE: OUR DEBT PAID

*Debt* and *penalty* are accounting terms used to show us the books are not cleared, the debt must be paid. (Like the Visa bill!) When a debt is paid, the person is excused, forgiven. When paid for by another person, this is called "grace."

**One person can take the punishment for another person.**

The Bible uses the word "grace" repeatedly to explain the cross. "The grace of God that brings salvation has appeared to all men" (Titus 2:11). "We are justified freely by his grace through the redemption that came by Christ Jesus" (Rom. 3:24).

A sad but true story gives us a picture of grace through the cross. Two men went to university together in Australia. One ultimately became a banker; the other, a lawyer and later a judge. Both men had brilliant careers. Twenty years passed and news came that the banker was charged with embezzling several million dollars. His case came up before the judge, his old college friend. What would the judge do? Because the defendant was his friend, would he be lenient in sentencing? Or would he, for fear of criticism, be overly tough?

The tension in the courtroom was high when the verdict of guilty was brought in. What would the final sentence be? The judge stood and read the maximum sentence that could be imposed: $1 million.

Unexpectedly, the spectators saw the judge rise, walk around the bench, take off his robe, and put his arm around his friend. He said, "I have sold my house and every one of my investments, and I will pay this debt for you." The man was free![12]

This was grace! The banker did nothing, earned nothing to pay his debt. The judge risked bankruptcy in order to pay the debt for his friend but also to ensure that justice would be carried out. At the same time, he showed his love for his friend. Such is the self-giving grace of God.

## NOT A PERFORMANCE KICK

After knowing the grace of God and forgiveness, it's easy to revert to a performance mentality. We think we still must earn God's grace. Our old mindset of hoping our good deeds outweigh our bad deeds stays with us. We forget we can never make heaven's standard on our own. We have no ability, no meritorious works to make it by ourselves; we need God's grace. We need the rescue operation of the cross. We cannot forget our magnificent connection with the One who gave all He had for our forgiveness.

"By grace you have been saved [forgiven], through faith—and this not from yourselves, it is the gift of God—not by works, so that no one can boast" (Eph. 2:8, 9).

After forgiving us, God forgets our misdeeds. We get a bonus, like the cherry on top of the ice cream sundae: besides forgiving, God does not remember our misdeeds. We are free! Repeat it over again. We are free! Author and pastor Tom Carter tells of a couple who were in the process of ironing out some communication problems. The wife said her husband always becomes "historical."

Tom interrupted her with "Don't you mean 'hysterical'?"

She answered sharply, "No, historical. He keeps bringing up my past."

The cross is definitely good news. A young woman in a study class read the verses I've listed below and the next week told the class, "This week has been the first time I went to sleep at night without feeling guilty. I know I am forgiven." God's relentless love for us is "without end." He doesn't torture us with our past failures. His words below reassure us.

**One God can take the punishment for every person on the planet.**

• As far as the east is from the west, so far has he removed our transgressions from us (Ps. 103:12).

• You have put all my sins behind your back (Isa. 38:17).

• I remember your sins no more (Isa. 43:25).

• You hurl all our iniquities into the depths of the sea (Micah 7:19).

• Look, the Lamb of God, who takes away the sin of the world (John 1:29).

• If we confess our sins, he is faithful and just and will forgive us our sins (1 John 1:29).

God's design makes the magnificent connection possible with the all-wise, holy God. Our part is to do as John Bunyan's Christian did: come to the cross for forgiveness. Then, like Christian, we can joyfully sing and give Him thanks.

## WRAP-UP #4: LOVE AND JUSTICE MEET

1. Explain what and by whom the "good news cross" originated.

2. How does Jesus' death on the cross fit the description "where love and justice meet"?

3. How do each of the following words or phrases shed light on the meaning of Jesus' death?

a. Earning versus a free gift

b. Grace

c. Good news

*He himself bore our sins in his body on the tree, so that we might die to sins and live for righteousness.*
—1 Pet. 2:24

# HE'S ALIVE

*In the Christian story,
God descends to earth,
then ascends to heaven.*

"The Rest of the Story" is a longtime radio program of newsman Paul Harvey, in which he fills out the fine details of an earlier story. For Jesus Christ, the rest of His story after the cross was a triumph, a crown of truth validating and confirming His identity as God incarnate.

To get a picture of the story, suppose I were to say to you after dinner, "You know, it has nothing to do with the food tonight, but I don't feel well, and as a matter of fact, I feel as if I'm going to pass out and expire about midnight. But don't worry about getting a substitute to teach. I'll be back in three days. Whatever your reaction might be, if you thought I was serious, it would not be "So what else is new?"

Five times in the course of His life, Jesus specifically predicted He was going to die (Mark 8:31; Mark 10:32-34; Matt. 16:21; Matt. 17:22-23; Luke.9:22). He described in detail His crucifixion and told how three days later He would rise from the dead and come back. The impact of this announcement from Him can be lost to us in this twenty-first century.

When Jesus foretold His coming destiny to the disciples, their reactions were mixed. It was not unusual for them to be mystified by some of His statements. Sometimes they protested, sometimes not. Looking back, we now know the events He described came about exactly as He said. Jesus was crucified and in three days came out of the tomb. Today, the accuracy of these events has become the strongest evidence to establish Christianity as a historical, nonmythological faith. The resurrection happened within the verifiable warp and woof of human history.

The resurrection is at the top of the list of reasons for recognizing Jesus' Godship. It validates His identity, His deity, His miracles, His power over nature, His hand in creating us and our world. The resurrection confirms His compassion for each one of us, His creation.

## THE STORY

All four Gospels of the New Testament tell this incredible story. Jesus and His disciples were praying in the Garden of Gethsemane. A cadre of Roman soldiers sent from the chief priests, the teachers of the law, and the Hebrew elders captured Him. After a series of trials during that night, at six o'clock in the morning the soldiers took Him outside the city of Jerusalem to the hill of Golgotha to be crucified. No more cruel death can be imagined; nails were put into both hands and feet and He was nailed to a wooden cross. Death came through asphyxiation.

Jesus died before sunset Friday afternoon, and two of His disciples took His body to a newly carved tomb, wrapped Him like a mummy in linen, and poured on seventy-five pounds of spices! (John 19:39) Such a large amount of spices was normally used in only royal burials. Then a heavy stone weighing several tons was rolled across the opening by the Roman soldiers. These rock-hewn tombs in Palestine usually closed with a circular stone set in a slanting groove. When pushed, by its own weight it would close the door. Several strong men would be needed to remove it.

Jesus' enemies, the religious leaders, were not going to take any chances. Fearing the disciples might steal the body, they asked for a Roman seal to be placed on the stone entrance as a sign of Roman authority. In their paranoia they also asked for a cadre of Roman soldiers to guard the seal (and the tomb) around the clock.

That was late Friday afternoon. Then three days later (the Sunday we call Easter) the heavy stone had been rolled aside and the tomb was empty. Jesus had come out of the grave—He was alive, not dead! This was His final triumph, His authentication that He was not an ordinary man, not a run-of-the-mill prophet. More than that, He was the God who conquered death. This begins the rest of His true story.

## HOW DID THE TOMB GET EMPTY?

On Sunday morning, three days after the burial, several women (and later two men) who were followers of Jesus came to the tomb and found the tomb open, the stone rolled away from the entrance, the body gone, and the tomb empty. The guards must have had fled in terror. The religious leaders were desperate to hide this mysterious event. They doled out a large sum of money to keep the soldiers quiet and told them, "Tell everybody the disciples stole the body while you were asleep."

This would be like reporting to the police your wallet was missing and telling them your neighbor across the hall came in and took it while you were sleeping. Does anyone know what happens while they sleep? The hypocrisy of the whole situation evidently didn't occur to these men. All His enemies wanted to do was explain away Jesus' power and denigrate Him.

If the Resurrection didn't happen and the record of it is a fable, no one has come up with a plausible explanation for these historic events. For more than two thousand years, a number of possibilities have been proposed by honest doubters without success.

The "swoon theory" was one popular story spread around without much success. David Strauss, a German skeptic, exploded this theory neatly. He wrote:

"To conceive of a man hanging on a Roman cross in a blistering sun for six hours, a spear put through his side, taken down from a cross and wrapped like a mummy, as was their custom, sealed into a tomb without air, that such a person could have found his way out of this, rolled away a stone of more than a ton, fought his way past a Roman guard and appeared as a hero eight miles away to his disciples is more fantastic than the resurrection itself!"[13]

## ENEMIES OR DISCIPLES?

Another rumor posited that the enemies of Jesus stole the body. The details of their carrying this out without being discovered by soldiers and mourners would be a problem. Besides, since they wanted Jesus destroyed, they could easily demolish all His claims by parading down the main street of Jerusalem with His dead body. Then they could say, "See, what He predicted was a lie; He's dead." Enemies stealing it evokes no sense of validity at all.

What if the disciples stole the body? Circumstantial evidence unquestionably points away from this. The two women who first discovered the tomb was empty were carrying spices to anoint the dead body! When Jesus appeared to one of them in the garden, she jumped with fright, not recognizing Him. Furthermore, in years of research and archeological digging, no dead body has ever been produced. Scores of people have tried with avid determination to prove this possibility without success.

## THE DISCIPLES HALLUCINATED?

I was in college when I first heard about the "hallucination theory"to explain away this miracle. For a moment it sounded plausible to me. To have a hallucination, I learned, people must so intensely want to believe something that they ruminate on it, are absorbed with it, project it, and attach a reality to it until finally they accept it as wholly true.

The bottom-line requirement for hallucination is an intense, impassioned desire to believe, regardless of the facts. This kind of evidence was demonstrably absent from the record of the disciples' lives. Further, large groups of people have never been known to have the same hallucination. At least one of the followers would have been honest enough to see through it, especially when as many as five hundred people saw Jesus in His resurrected body at one time.

Doubting Thomas, the classic example of unbelief, was openly skeptical about the reports from other disciples. On hearing their reports, Thomas told them, "Unless I see in his hands the print of the nails, place my finger in that mark, and place my hand in his side, I will not believe" (John 20:25). Thomas wasn't about to have a hallucination! His first reaction was the honest "Alive? Nothing doing! I'm an empiricist; I go only by empirical evidence. I won't believe until I see for myself."

Eight days later Jesus appeared unannounced to a group of disciples, looked them squarely in the eyes, and said, "Peace be with you." Right away He turned to Thomas, "Put your finger here and see my hands; and place your hand in my side. Don't be faithless, but be believing." It was the same body, the same crucified Jesus, the scars still there. It was a resurrected body, there was no doubt. All doubts erased, Thomas fell to his knees and cried, "My Lord and my God!" (John 20:28). This first-hand encounter changed his entire life. He is now known as the great evangelist who spent his life preaching about Jesus in India.

In another of Jesus' twelve recorded appearances, He came to the disciples on the shore of the Sea of Galilee. The men were startled because they thought they had seen a ghost. "Fear shook them," the text says. But Jesus said gently, "Why are you troubled? See my hands and feet, it is I, myself." His next words were, "Do you have anything to eat?" They gave Him a piece of broiled fish and He ate with them. Luke, the author, doesn't point out the obvious—ghosts don't eat fish! This certainly was the same Jesus.

The experience of Thomas was duplicated by many others in their first encounters with Him. Today in our courts, two or three witnesses are accepted as adequate to validate truth.

> **The earliest converts came to Christ after a single historical fact, the Resurrection, and a single historical doctrine, Redemption.**
>
> *C. S. Lewis*

## WHIMPERING HE-MEN TO ROARING LIONS

The hallucination theory fits none of the responses of the other disciples. Some had been so frightened at the time Jesus was arrested that they huddled together in fear. Peter, a notoriously outspoken personality, told three different people he never knew Jesus! Roman soldiers had them all cowed. But the hard facts of seeing the risen Christ revolutionized the small band of disciples and the 120 followers who joined them.

The truth of the Resurrection transformed these whimpering he-men into roaring lions. Peter stood and preached the Resurrection in downtown Jerusalem, the very place where he had denied Jesus fifty days before. Three thousand people believed his message that day and subsequently were baptized. Peter had the newfound courage to tell them truthfully, "This same Jesus, whom you crucified, God has raised from the dead, whereby we have become eye witnesses" (Acts 2:36).

The apostle Paul documents several post-Resurrection appearances: "Christ died for our sins ... was raised on the third day ... he appeared to Peter, and then to the Twelve. After that, He appeared to more than

51

five hundred of the brothers at the same time, most of whom are still living ... Then He appeared to James, then to all the apostles, and last of all to me" (1 Cor. 15:3-8). Paul also puts his finger on the importance of the Resurrection: "And if Christ has not been raised, our preaching is useless and so is your faith!" (1 Cor. 15:14).

The events are convincing that the resurrection of Jesus Christ is not a mere spiritual resurrection, implying that Jesus lives on in spirit. It is not like Beethoven or Mozart live on through their music. Jesus Christ rose physically from the grave; it was a bodily resurrection, as the events uphold and support. He is alive today!

The Resurrection has been called the best-attested fact of ancient history. It is possible to visit the graves of other religious leaders; but the only empty one belongs to Jesus. The literal bodily resurrection of Christ is the only conclusion that adequately explains the history of the first century. His empty tomb stands more than two thousand years later as the immovable base of the Christian faith.

### WE CAN CONNECT, HE IS ALIVE!

Talk to Him? Connect with Him? Of course. "We have many infallible proofs," Luke wrote in Acts 1:3. At the end of the fourth Gospel, John tells us Jesus did many other things as well and if they were written, the whole world would not have room for the books that would contain them.

> **Jesus' resurrection was a *bodily* resurrection, not a "spiritual" appearance or a vision. Jesus ate boiled fish!**

52

• Jesus Christ's life, death, and Resurrection finalize His purpose to rescue us. He accepted the disciples where they were and transformed them, and likewise He accepts us and extends His Resurrection power to us. His Resurrection authenticates His power to transform. When Peter was asked, "By what power or what name were these men made whole?" he gave a straightforward answer. "It is by the name of Jesus Christ whom you crucified, but whom God raised from the dead" (Acts 4:10).

He died and rose again "so as to be just and the one who justifies those who have faith in Jesus" (Rom. 3:26).

"He set aside the privileges of deity ... and took on the status of a slave, became human!" (Phil. 2:7, *The Message*).

• He has power over death and gives us eternal life.

"Jesus said, I am the Resurrection and the Life; he who believes in me, though He die, yet shall he live" (John 11:25).

"You pinned Him to a cross and killed him. But God untied the death ropes and raised him up. Death was no match for him" (Acts 2:23, 24).

• Jesus' life, death, and resurrection are proof of how much God values each one of us. John described it: "This is how God showed his love among us: He sent his one and only Son into the world that we might live through him" (1 John 4:9).

Today and tomorrow, look up to Him, talk to Him. He's alive!

## WRAP-UP #5: HE'S ALIVE!

1. Explain which evidences for the Resurrection you found most convincing.

2. When doubts arise, how can the strong historical, nonmythological evidences help your thinking?

3. When you pray, how can these evidences help direct your prayer?

53

*"In his great mercy [God] has given us new birth into a living hope through the resurrection of Jesus Christ from the dead."*
—1 Pet. 1:3

# JESUS CHRIST,
# A VALID OBJECT

*The word* faith *makes a lot of people nervous.*
*It seems foggy, anti-intellectual,*
*superstitious.*

An airplane rocks precariously, a sickening thud signals engine trouble, altitude is lost, seat belt lights are flashing, the pilot signals the control tower anxiously. Finally, the runway becomes visible and the pilot skillfully taxis to a merciful halt. The passengers and crew are safe.

The pilot is swamped with "How did you do it?" He answers, "Well, we came in by faith." Everybody gets a vague, mystical feeling. No one is quite certain what he means, but whatever "faith" is, it did work. Used in this way, "faith" probably means the pilot trusted his own skill and self-control.

Or someone is about to flunk out of school and a friend slaps him on the back and says, "That's all right, just have faith." Here, it may be a word of cheer and no more. Good luck, ole boy! Try your best. Other expressions such as having faith in your fellow man, your country, and your future can be used merely as soothing aphorisms.

When it comes to the Christian faith, some people would like to have faith in Jesus Christ but "just can't believe." They probably mean,

"I've got a little bit too much upstairs in the brain, and I can't be quite that naive. It must be wonderful to be that simpleminded, but I'm not." Underneath the common usage of faith is the ambiguous assumption that it doesn't matter what you believe as long as you have this mystical thing called faith. This usage also carries the idea that it is necessary to abandon all reason, all logical thinking. Believe something you know isn't true!

A man sat in the park reading a paperback book, and as he read each page, he ripped it out, tore it up in little pieces, and scattered them around the bench. He did this with page after page until a policeman observing him came up and said, "Sir, apart from the fact that you're littering, I wonder if you would mind telling me why, after you read each page, you tear it out and scatter it on the ground?"

The fellow brightened and said, "Sure, it's to keep the elephants away."

"To keep the elephants away? I don't see any elephants."

The fellow responded, "Pretty effective, isn't it?"

If faith is as divorced from reality as tearing paper to "keep the elephants away," no wonder there are questions. A true understanding of faith turns on our definition of it.

> Connecting
> with God
> is more
> satisfying
> than
> answers
> proposed
> without
> God.

## THE OBJECT OF YOUR FAITH

For faith in general and the Christian faith specifically, five observations help.

*First, faith is no more valid than the object in which it is placed.*

Suppose you have a neighbor who's been a very good friend and he comes to you one afternoon and says, "I would like to borrow $50 from you." You've always thought of him as a good friend (maybe not that good, but basically a good friend), so you give him $50. He doesn't tell you he lost his job the day before and he's planning to leave town that night, never to return. Good-bye fifty dollars! You had faith in him, but in this case, it was no more than unfounded trust. An invalid object.

Some of the great Christian heroes in history have been called men and women of great faith. What qualified them for this compliment? They trusted a great God. The object of their faith was a powerful and personal God. The biblical story of Daniel enduring the lion's den tells of a man who didn't doubt for a moment that God the Creator of the universe was One he could trust. Daniel's enemies created a law requiring people to pray only to King Darius in order to catch Daniel praying to his God. That didn't stop Daniel. He prayed to God anyway, so he was put into a den of lions.

Daniel spent the night facing lions, and in the morning, completely unharmed, he was brought out by the king. Talk about impressed! Darius decreed Daniel's God to be "the living God ... One who rescues and saves." It's easy to see what Daniel would tell us today. It wasn't his great faith that saved him; those lions were hungry. It was his great God. Daniel didn't have an emaciated, haggard, weak God who was getting artificial respiration. The object of his faith was unquestionably valid. (You can read the whole story in Daniel 6.)

The story of a desperately anxious parent in a primitive culture speaks to this point. A father had a seriously ill child with a high fever and needed help. The only doctor available was a witch doctor who gave him a potion of his own concoction without any pharmaceutical base. It was poison. The parent had implicit faith in the potion, but sadly, his faith couldn't save his daughter. The object of his faith was invalid. He might as well have had faith in a flower, a stone, or a puff of smoke. So we need to ask ourselves a crucial question: Is the object of our faith valid (reliable)?

*Second, believing something does not make it true.* I have seen some people devote their entire lives to imagined truth. However intense their belief may be, faith does not create truth. If someone believes a hamburger is free of the mad-cow virus and eats it even though it is contaminated, the truth will come out. "Just eat it!" All the faith in the world isn't going to keep that person from getting sick. Intensity of belief, however immovable, does not make a thing true. Faith does not change untruth to truth!

In the area of spiritual belief, this is crucial. (Extreme examples of invalid objects in our day are the likes of Jim Jones, David Koresh, or Japanese cult leader Aum Shinri, who gassed the Tokyo trains. Each one convinced people of his validity.) A kind of emotional blackmail can convince us of some newly revealed truth. The most seductive ingredient can be some euphoric, emotional experience peddling an invalid truth claim. It can be very aluring.

These beliefs can be on the level of the man we meet with a

peeled banana hanging on his ear. In his intense belief he claims it gives him peace, joy, and bliss. We would be quick to ask him who else has had this experience and what proof can be produced for its origin and authenticity. He intensely believes it is true!

*Third, not believing something doesn't make it untrue.* Recently a neighbor said to me, "Oh, I don't believe in God or Jesus Christ." University students, Wall Street bankers, or salespersons might honestly say this. Does this wipe out the existence of God? Of course not. If a person has never heard an intelligent rationale for believing in the Christian faith, this is an understandable conclusion, but it doesn't disprove it. A number of well-known scholars have documented and published their sincere attempt to disprove the Christian basics, and after examining the wealth of objective evidence, they have ended up as strong apologists for believing.

A poverty-stricken recluse in Texas—one of those people with cats running all over the place and newspapers stuffed everywhere—was informed he had inherited a million dollars from a relative in England whom he didn't even realize existed. It was a fact—the recluse was heir to a million dollars—but tragically he didn't believe it and died a starving old man. His unbelief robbed him of the enjoyment of his wealth.

Faith enables us to enter into the reality of that which is already true. It doesn't create truth out of something that is not objectively true already. There's nothing spooky about the word *faith*; it simply means to trust what is demonstrably true.

*Fourth, faith is something that every one of us uses every day.* We all exercise reasonable faith every day. When we go to a restaurant, we eat food that we didn't see prepared. We eat the food in blind faith, and just how blind our faith is we may never know unless we go behind the scenes. (If we did see it prepared, we might not eat it!) We usually don't drop like flies from ptomaine poisoning in our favorite restaurant. But we exercise faith when we choose to eat there.

Other examples are myriad. We go to the pharmacist, the doctor, the teacher, the banker, the auto dealer and believe in them. The student who enrolls in a college exercises faith in that college; he assumes that after completing a certain series of course requirements he will be awarded a degree. If he thought that this year the institution would suddenly say, "Well, we don't want to be conformists, so this year we're not going to award any degrees," he would change schools immediately. Certainly, a student would check out a school.

Likewise, we would check out whatever we place our faith in.

When I first learned I had a heart condition and it possibly could be corrected by surgery, I read everything about the condition I could get my hands on. I read the medical journals in the library. I remember one scholarly, eight-page article that ended, "We can therefore conclude, in the light of data thus far, that there are basically three results of heart surgery: one, marked improvement; two, no improvement; three, death." *Well,* I thought to myself, *that was tremendously profound!* I'd had that suspicion myself before I read the article; now I had it confirmed by scientific data.

After all the reading, I checked out the surgeon's record and talked to people who had had the surgery. Then I was convinced that I should go ahead with it. I still had to exercise faith. My reason took me to an understanding, then I took the step and put my faith in a proven expert. If I'd had all the information and had stopped there, I would still have the heart condition today. The doctor told me, "If you continue without surgery, in ten to fifteen years your heart will continue to enlarge and then collapse."

**Faith is a living, daring, confident trust in God's grace. It is a choice, an act of belief.**

*Fifth, faith goes beyond reason but not against reason.* Fortunately, my faith went beyond my reason. I committed my life to that surgeon. I exercised reasonable faith, since all the data pointed in that direction. Faith, then, goes beyond reason.

As in the case of my surgery, faith in the reasonableness of Christianity is an act, a choice. Faith goes beyond reason but not against reason. The "leap of faith" (as it has been called) is a decision. Viewing the large body of rational information about God and Jesus Christ, we move to place our faith in them. There may be some things we do not fully understand, but after thinking carefully about the evidence that is obvious and reasonable, I can take the step of faith and be certain of it.

Is Christianity credible? Yes. Christianity is the most credible experience and life system, and it gives us the key to meaning in the universe. When we decide to place our faith in Jesus Christ, we find from the abundance of trustworthy historical data and from the countless personal experiential data that He is a valid object: an object—a Person—we can confidently believe in.

The real question is not whether one person has faith and another person doesn't; the beginning question is whether the object of our faith is worth trusting. In the previous five chapters we have laid a foundation for answering questions like "Is Jesus Christ a valid object for my faith? Is He truly God come to earth? Is He trustworthy? Is He someone to whom I can commit myself with confidence today?"

An Oxford University professor described his faith journey. "I was traveling on the top of a bus when without words and almost without images, a fact about myself was somehow presented to me. I became aware that I was holding something at bay, or shutting something out. Or, if you like, that I was wearing some stiff clothing, like corsets, or even a suit of armor, as if I were a lobster. I felt myself being, there and then, given a free choice.

"I could open the door or keep it shut; I could unbuckle the armor or keep it on. Neither choice was presented as a duty; no threat or promise was attached to either, though I knew to open the door or to take off the corset meant the incalculable. ... I chose to open, to unbuckle, to loosen the rein. I say 'I chose,' yet it did not really seem possible to do otherwise."

So it was that C. S. Lewis describes taking his leap of faith in his absorbing autobiography *Surprised by Joy*.[14]

## THE STRONG PLANK THEORY

A simple test I've found for making faith work is the strong plank theory. If you are going to cross a small stream without getting wet, you might be tempted to try a weak, narrow plank and hope it will take you across. Faith in that weak plank could be invincible, unwavering, but also invalid, and you could land in the creek. On the other hand, if you can find a really strong plank, your faith may be weak and skeptical by this time, not certain about getting across. The plank is strong; you will make it. Whatever or whoever you are trusting for your life, make certain your faith is in a strong, valid plank!

Strong faith in a weak plank is invalid faith.

Weak faith in a strong plank is valid faith.

The Christian faith is a strong, proven plank that has been confirmed objectively and does not defy reason. Jesus Christ is undeniably true because of the objective historic facts we know of His life, death, and resurrection. Personal experiences with Him have confirmed the reality of His presence and power. In the laboratory of life, Jesus Christ invites each of us to validate His claims for ourselves. The real dynamic of Christianity is that, today, He offers to connect with anyone who will respond to Him. We can find for ourselves in personal experience that He is a strong, reliable plank for our lives. The apostle Peter gives a cryptic summary of faith:

"We did not follow cleverly invented stories when we told you about the power and coming of our Lord Jesus Christ, but we were eyewitnesses of his majesty" (2 Pet. 1:16).

## WRAP-UP #6: JESUS CHRIST, A VALID OBJECT

1. Why is it helpful to investigate objective evidence for God and Jesus Christ?

2. What are some helpful sources to acquire needed evidence?

3. How do belief and action differ in the step of faith?

61

*"Love the Lord your God with all your heart and with all your soul and with all your mind."*
—Matt. 22:37

# MAKING THE MAGNIFICENT CONNECTION

*The Gospel is not what we can do for ourselves but what God stands ready to do for us.*

The sub-title *The Magnificent Connection* first came to my mind as I rehearsed the heart-thumping meaning of Jesus' bold words: "I am the Door." "I am the Way." "I am the Truth." "I am the Life." "I will give you rest." He offers a connection to all who will respond to Him. Jesus exact words were: "Here I am! I stand at the door and knock. If anyone hears my voice and opens the door, I will come in and eat with him, and he with me" (Rev. 3:20).

If we own and ruminate on the meaning of Jesus' offer, it can take a while to digest it. It can be staggering and life changing. He offers us an unexcelled and uncommon relationship, a one-on-one personal connection to the God of the universe. It's an offer we'd be foolish to refuse. A few of the benefits come to mind immediately:

- Security and new life in our inner spirit
- Divine wisdom for hard choices
- Purpose to each day instead of aimlessness
- Forgiveness and freedom from sinful habits

- Freedom from guilt
- Peace of heart in spite of disappointments
- Divine encouragement from His promises
- Inner strength to endure one day at a time
- Joy from His steady companionship

Jesus promises, "Whoever drinks of the water I give him will never thirst. Indeed, the water I give him will become in him a spring of water welling up to eternal life" (Luke 4:14).

Sara and John were a young couple who lived next door to us for seven or eight years. As we talked over a redwood fence time after time, we exchanged a whole book full of life stories. One day, Sara said, "My religion doesn't mean as much to me as yours does to you." We asked her and her husband to join us in a couples' study group in our neighborhood. About the fifth time she came, Sara asked for prayer for a guilt that had plagued her for years. She said, "I don't know what to pray." We knelt around a coffee table and we all prayed she would know the forgiveness that Jesus offers.

A few days later, Sara asked us what happened to her that night. "I feel peace now. I didn't have it before," she said. One of our prized possessions is a note she wrote us with the line "Thank you for introducing me to Jesus, and I didn't even *know who* I was looking for!" She went through the door, forgiven, and began this magnificent connection with Jesus Christ. Before, she believed in a God. Now she knows God!

"So, chosen by God for this new life of love, dress in the wardrobe God picked out for you: compassion, kindness, humility, quiet strength, discipline. Be even tempered, content with second place, quick to forgive an offense. Forgive as quickly and completely as the Master forgave you. And regardless of what else you put on, wear love. It's your basic, all-purpose garment. Never be without it" (Col. 3:12–14, *The Message*).

One businessman in his vernacular explained entering the door as "getting suited up" with Jesus Christ. The New Testament uses the illustration of marriage to describe opening the door in commitment.

For instance, suppose you know a young man or woman and you really believe in this person, are drawn to him or her. You are convinced this person is the greatest. This person has integrity, character, and beauty and understands us. You are really convinced about this person intellectually. The most on either coast; you name it, this one has it. Does all this make you married to that person? Of course not. Some of us rather wish it would. Marriage takes a little more than that.

One more thing is absolutely necessary. A commitment of the will, an act of faith is necessary. We name a time and place and we each say a clear "I do." By a specific act, we receive that person into our lives, we establish a lifelong connection, we are married! After the connection is made, we begin to see life through different lenses. We are together, we are one.

There are distinct similarities between getting married and beginning a relationship with Jesus Christ. An "I do" is also needed with Him. John 1:12 helps us get unstuck and through the door to make this uncommon connection. "To all who *received* him, to those who *believed* in his name, he gave the right to *become* children of God" (emphasis added).

**The Gospel is not what we can do for ourselves but what God stands ready to do for us.**

## BASICS TO GET THROUGH THE DOOR

a. We believe the truth Jesus Christ spoke of Himself and God: His deity, His character, and His sacrifice on the cross.

"The Word became flesh and made his dwelling among us" (John 1:14).

"I tell you the truth, no one can see the kingdom of God unless he is born again" (John 3:3).

b. We receive Him and tell Him we want Him to direct us in every area of our lives. A suggested prayer: "I do take You, Jesus Christ, into my life. I give You all that I am. Forgive my wrongdoing of every kind. Give me Your power to change. Thank You for Your deep, sacrificing love and Your holy character. Thank You for making forgiveness possible by Your death on the cross."

c. He gives us the right to become children of God. He gives us the privilege of knowing we belong to Him. We are His children: Christians! We made the connection.

"Yet to all who received him, to those who believed in his name, he gave the right to become children of God" (John 1:12).

Again, in this action, we open every area of our lives to Him for His directorship. If we have never prayed before in an audible or specific way, we may feel awkward at first. But like the "I do" in a wedding ceremony, we make this an honest, wholehearted commitment for life. The prayer can be very simple, and when said in above-board honesty, we are opening the door to a life-enriching relationship with God.

God responds instantly and new life from Him begins: a life of connecting constantly, consulting, sharing, believing. Remember, when we walk through the door, Jesus Christ Himself is there waiting.

## SPIRITUAL LIFE IS NEW

Once inside the door, incredible benefits wait for us. It is true, in one sense we are all children of God by creation; He made us. That creation gave us natural life. Jesus' stated reason for coming to earth was to give us spiritual life, a one-on-one personal connection with Himself. We do not go through the natural birth process again; however, we receive a divine Person and His brand-new, supernatural life. This is spiritual transformation; we have come from death to life. C. S. Lewis describes it:

"What man, in his natural condition, does not have is spiritual life—the higher and different sort of life that exists in God. ... And that is precisely what faith in Jesus Christ is about. This world is a great sculptor's shop. We are the statues and there is a rumor going round the shop that some of us are some day going to come to life. ... Christ making New Men is like turning a horse into a winged creature. It is not mere improvement but transformation!" (C. S. Lewis, *Mere Christianity*).[15]

## TWO SMALL WORDS

Lewis surely thought of the apostle Paul's words: "Therefore, if anyone is in Christ, he is a new creation; the old has gone, the new has come!" (2 Cor. 5:17). Making the connection and joining to Jesus Christ creates a genuine inner change. In the everyday reality of life, there is a new awareness of God, a new power and center. In some cases, it may be as dramatic as a concrete statue coming to life or a horse turning into a winged creature, as Lewis described it.

> **To believe and to pray is the beginning of making the Connection.**

This is not turning over a new leaf or trying to follow the example of Christ. We don't get to be a doctor by putting on a white coat. He is alive; He comes and lives in us by His Holy Spirit. When Jesus Christ is in us, we will sense an unbeatable stability. Inside, we see our worldview and our self-view through His lenses.

The new creation that Paul speaks of is divine life, God's Holy Spirit living within us, bringing His power and purpose to us. When we sense His presence and joy, it is His Spirit transforming our inner life to newness. "The Spirit Himself testifies with our spirit that we are God's children" (Rom. 8:16).

Jesus said this new life is being born again of the Spirit (John 3:8). God does not make good people better but spiritually dead people alive—alive to Him. The old dead impulses are gone, and "the new has come." A whole new awareness of God, new reasons to live, new joys to experience, new power to be free and clean inside. With Him, all is new.

### IT'S NOT HOW WE FEEL

As children of God we are not always going to feel exuberant. Some days we can say, "Today I feel like I'm a Christian." Tomorrow we may not feel like it. If we wake up in the morning with a headache, the toast is burned, the scrambled eggs are sour, and our roommate is grouchy, we don't feel like much of anything. Our assurance of a relationship with Christ could be blown to bits if it were based on emotional highs.

The certainty and assurance that we have become children of God cannot rest on how we feel but rather on God's promises. Let's say I've had sixteen meetings in three days, and students have been talking to me until three in the morning, and somebody comes to me and says, "Do you feel married?" I would have to say I don't feel like much of anything except sleep. "Do you know you're married?" I say, "Sure, I know I'm married." I know I'm married because at a particular time and place I committed myself to my wife and she to me. We established a permanent relationship. Similarly, the abiding relationship with Jesus never changes.

You may have heard the old proverb of Mr. Fact, Mr. Faith, and Mr. Feeling. Mr. Fact, Mr. Faith, and Mr. Feeling were walking along a very narrow wall. As long as Mr. Faith kept his eye on Mr. Fact, Mr. Feeling followed right along with beautiful progress. But every time Mr. Faith turned around and looked at Mr. Feeling, they almost fell off, because they forgot the facts and were paralyzed with fear. Certainty of salvation and new life rests in the fact of God's revealed Son, who is the door to this magnificent connection. Open the door and wonderful feelings will follow.

## WE CAN KNOW

The New Testament emphasizes that our relationship with God through Jesus Christ is unending and eternal. Referring to the certainty of our relationship with Him, the book of 1 John uses the word *know* twenty-six times. Chapter 2 starts with "We know that we know Him" 1 John 5:13 summarizes, "I write ... so that you may know that you have eternal life."

It's not prideful to say I know I am a Christian. Pride in no way enters into the picture. Our knowing is simply taking God at His Word, believing God has spoken the truth. To open the door is the dignity of choice God gives us; all we do is answer the door to Him. Then He gives us the right to be called children of God.

Further, our new life has one focal point: Jesus Christ Himself. His new life is of such value that all else pales by comparison. It does not necessarily bring a high grade point average, health, wealth, and a late-model car. Far greater than external things is the reality that we are never alone. It is wise to remember this when times get hard. We are joined with our divine Shepherd.

Being sure of our relationship with Jesus Christ and being certain of our future does not mean that we can develop a careless attitude toward life and sin. I've had people say to me, "Well, if you're sure you have eternal life and will be in the presence of God, that means there's no incentive to live a good life. You could live as you please!"

This might seem to be true on the surface. However, it would be like saying, "I'm certain I'm married, so now I can date anybody else." (That marriage wouldn't last, we know.) In thinking of this, one vital fact is overlooked: when a personal relationship with Jesus Christ is established, an internal revolution takes place within the life of the person. A true view of the heavenly Artist heightens our desire to get closer and know Him more deeply. He brings anticipation of a great life He has for us: "He makes me lie down in green pastures" (Ps. 23:2).

## OPEN THE DOOR

Jesus Christ issues the invitation. He will never gate-crash. His offer is what we are all secretly looking for. John Stott suggests:

He is standing patiently—not kicking it.

He is knocking gently—not pushing it.

He is speaking softly—not shouting.[16]

Our part is to open the door. It is this step that answers the question we posed at the beginning of the book: What makes a person a Christian?

When we open the door of our lives to Jesus Christ in genuine honesty, we make the connection. That act is our "new birth." We can say we are Christians. Significantly, Jesus politely stands waiting. A simple, wholehearted initiative, a prayer, and even giving thanks to Him will bring instant response. Remember, He says, if you open the door, "I will come in and will eat with him and he with me" (Rev. 3:20). Sealed with His words "I will be with you always" (Matt. 28:20), you will have made the unbeatable beginning by making the magnificent connection! Think of it. You'll know God personally!

## WRAP-UP #7: MAKE THE MAGNIFICENT CONNECTION

1. Now we arrive at the summit, the Door, Jesus Christ Himself. Rehearse the three operative verbs in John 1:12:

a.

b.

c.

2. On what basis can you know with certainty that you are a Christian?

3. Explain your understanding of "new creation" and "new life in Christ."

*Jesus says, "I have come that they may have life, and have it to the full."*
—John 10:10

# GOD
# USES WORDS

*The Bible is not intended only for scholars.
From the beginning it was intended to be
everybody's book. (F. F. Bruce)*

The vocalist stood up in church and sang this first line: "When God speaks, the high mountains tremble." The lyrics went on praising the potency of God speaking to us, then ended with "And there is response in my soul!" Unexpectedly, the remark a student made earlier flared in my mind, "Whenever I read the Bible, I fall asleep." The contrast woke me up, to say the least, and I don't want to forget the subtle warning.

Not sleep, but trembling, would be a more appropriate response to the Bible, this world's bestseller. Think of it: our Creator God revealing His thoughts to us! At the very least, it should grab our attention. This book is God's self-revelation in which He tells us about Himself. It is also His personal message to each of us.

We all like to receive news from our family or loved ones. Isn't checking the mail one of the first things you do when you come into the house? It is no exaggeration to say the Bible is God's letter to us, giving us His thoughts and waiting for our response.

The people in the Bible who heard God speak were anything but sleepy. They described God's Word as:

| | |
|---|---|
| Honey to the taste | A sword that cuts |
| Spiritual food for the hungry | Sharp as a two-edged sword |
| A guide for the feet | Flawless |
| Enlightens the mind | Dwells in us richly |
| A fire that burns the heart | The joy and delight of the heart |
| Spurs us to preach | A hammer that breaks a rock in |
| A lamp to the path | pieces |

The Bible is not an ordinary textbook or philosophic treatise. It is called the "Word of God" 3,808 times in the Old Testament. And the New Testament uses quotes from the Old Testament as the "Word of God." The psalmist zeroed in with, "I have hidden your word in my heart that I might not sin against you" (Ps. 119:11). This psalm is a model of literary genius, referring to the "Word of God" with an alphabetic acrostic, devoting eight verses to each of the twenty-one letters of the Hebrew alphabet—a total of 176 verses. In each of these verses, all but one refers to the "Word of God" in some form or another.

## ONE SINGLE THEME

This extraordinary book, although written by about forty authors, shows a single theme: God linking to people, and their response. This thread is woven through every book from beginning to end. The earliest book was authored about 1500 B.C. and the last one, Revelation, was finished about one hundred years after Jesus' birth—a span of about 1,600 years. Although about forty authors were involved, one theme continues. The first book begins when God put the "tree of life" into the Garden of Eden (Gen. 2:9); the final book tells us where that tree is now—in heaven, where all tears will be washed away (Rev. 22:1–3).

Jesus used the Old Testament as His sourcebook on many occasions, particularly in His conflict in the wilderness with Satan. "It is written" was His usual phrase. In John 10:35 He uses the blanket statement "the Scripture cannot be broken."

**Reading the Bible with understanding is like eating peanuts: the more you eat, the more you want to eat.**

The historical accuracy or historicity of the Bible has been affirmed by an astonishing number of archaeological digs. Whole nations and people groups known only through the Bible have later been found to exist through these digs, and many previously questioned names and places have been verified. The additional information has served to authenticate the Bible's truth and silence its critics.

Sir William Ramsey, originally an avowed skeptic, became a believing expert on life in New Testament times. His change of perspective started when he discovered the Book of Acts had differentiated two cities, Lycaonia and Iconium, even though most experts thought them to be one city. In his explorations he found a Roman arch that confirmed that the Acts record was correct after all. This experience spurred him on to uncover many more facts affirming the accuracy of the biblical record.[17]

## SMALL AIDS TO UNDERSTANDING

One very common question, and an important one, is "Should we take the Bible literally or figuratively?" In common, everyday speech, we solve this problem without thinking. "I was angry as a mad dog." "I was tired to death." "She sang like a bird." Obviously we interpret the meaning behind these statements. In reading the Bible, there are a few guidelines.

• Recognize figures of speech by questioning the intent of the author. Look through his eyes for his meaning. The Bible is replete with metaphors, such as a door and vine and branches. Obviously, these are figurative, not wooden, doors or literal plants.

• Consider the context, the people involved, the situation, the culture of those to whom it was written, and the perspective of the writer. How would the original readers have understand the words?

• The Bible describes things phenomenologically—that is, as things appear to the eye—both ordinary things and extraordinary things. We do the same. It appears to us that the sun rises, yet we all know that the earth turns. When we get up early, we wouldn't say that we saw the earth turn; we would say we saw the sun rise! So finding similar expressions in the Bible doesn't mean the Bible is unscientific; rather, the authors are using ordinary language, just as we do. This principle also applies to other observable events. When the blind man was made to see by Jesus, for example, we have a normal eyewitness account. The common language doesn't allow us to interpret it as a vision or an allegory; the author was describing a real, observable event.

73

• There is a contrast between natural and supernatural events. The Bible shows the normal stability of nature, but it also assumes a powerful reality behind nature: God. And since God is greater than His creation, He can override natural laws and perform miracles, if He desires.

• Round numbers are often used in Scripture, as we'd find in a news report today.

• The Bible was meticulously preserved, copied from one manuscript to another, sometimes by two people, one letter at a time. There are some apparent minor differences, as in the spelling of a word or in the transcription or copying by the writers. (This was before the printing press.) The science of manuscript comparisons has shown the differences between the copies to be incredibly few. Its accuracy is nothing short of supernatural.

## STUDYING GOD'S LETTER

"Never study the Bible for purely academic purposes," said scholar Martin Lloyd-Jones.[19] Beyond its sacred pages, we connect personally to God, our Source. Academic understanding can help illumine our thoughts, but then the wise thing to do is speak to the Sender about it.

Rocker Boy George was quoted in *Servant Magazine* as saying, "Nothing outside yourself can make you feel whole. Not fame, not sex, not drugs, not money. None of these work. Nothing can fill you up. And believe me, 'cause I've tried them all." By contrast, Job, an Old Testament man, a man going through horrendous loss and suffering, said he treasured God's Word "more than my daily bread" (Job 23:12). In the midst of great sorrow, he fed on God's Word. For us, also, as food gets to the muscles and bloodstream, the words from God make us feel whole, satisfied, loved, connected—deep inside.[18]

Our faith is rooted in the Bible, but we do not worship it—we trust it. Our sole truth-source comes from its Author, God. Every new idea or even our emotional experiences are to be tested by the Bible's teachings. Today's world is soaked with spiritual gurus, trainers touting new visions, dreams, and experiences. Their charisma can mesmerize us. Their personal intentions may not be evil, but any experiences not congruent with the biblical record are not the Gospel, or Good News.

**The Bible is God's truth-source; it helps us think God's thoughts.**

The Bible spotlights the historic Jesus, the Messiah, foretelling His coming from the earliest chapters. The Bible is the written revelation of God and Jesus the Savior, the incarnation of God. His adequacy is our final binding authority. "All the prophets testify about him that everyone who believes in him receives forgiveness of sins through his name" (Acts 10:43).

Marianne, a mature woman in my class, heard that reading the Bible even fifteen minutes a day could change her life. She decided to find out for herself what this book had for her. The last I heard, she had read it through three times, with flags marked where questions came to her. What made her stand out was her accurate recall of new life lessons she learned and thorny issues she wanted to resolve. She could always remember where to find the verses. An example to all of us.

## LISTEN INTENTLY TO GOD'S MESSAGE

How we read God's mail can mean the difference between getting spiritual food and not getting spiritual food. Deliberate study of God's Word can mean the deepening of our faith, growing in the comprehension of God's ways, learning our Creator's ideas of structure for our lives, and showing us right principles for interpersonal decision making. There are many examples in each of these areas

Recently I was reading Galatians 6 and was struck with how contemporary the thoughts are. God's principles for interpersonal relationships are given specifically. Good counseling agrees with this detailed wisdom from God's perspective. Verses 1-5 tell how to help others, how to help ourselves, what to do when problems persist, and they end with this wise conclusion that each one of us is ultimately responsible for his or her own actions. I can't blame you and you can't blame me!

This is one small passage. A further sequence of study could be on the wisdom of Proverbs, the comfort of the Psalms, the creation of our world, or the intriguing self-control of Jesus in every situation. Most importantly, ingest and apply the thoughts; eat them as food for your soul. Jeremiah, like Job, ate God's Word and it became "my joy and my heart's delight" (Jer. 15:16). Peter tells us to eat God's Word so we will grow (1 Pet. 2:2). The psalmist said the absence of God's Word would bring "a wasting disease" (Ps. 106:15).

Let's be honest: have you ever read a chapter but can't remember one thing from it, let alone explain it to someone else? You are not alone. For this reason, it helps to regularly use a pen and a journal or notebook while reading.

One very simple habit I have is called The Three Rs of Bible Reading:

- *Read* the verses.

- *Reproduce* the ideas in your own words. Paraphrase.

- *Respond* to God about those thoughts. Pray to Him about what you have read.

To reproduce, munch on the words, probe the thoughts, rehearse them in your mind, apply them to your life. Question the meanings of individual words and probe ideas by asking questions such as who, what, when, and where. List the sequence of thoughts and ideas, expand and amplify them. If we remember only one thought that has gripped our hearts, we have made progress. The psalmist meditated on God's words "day and night" (Ps. 1:2). Take one thought from the text, make it your own, think on it all day.

To respond, always talk it over with God, the Author. The words are intended to bring conversation between us and Him. A conversation, by definition, is a two-way activity, with us listening and comprehending the other person's thoughts and then responding. This two-way interaction should help us delve into the character and thinking of our God. Define and memorize words that expand your knowledge of God. Your picture of God will be enlarged and new words will be added to your praise vocabulary.

## THE REWARDS

Most of us use our connection with God only as "Help!" He hears those cries day and night, and He is listening. But when we use the words and ideas we have reproduced and paraphrased, we will find our relationship with Him growing. Our trust in Him will be fortified and expanded with new words of praise and worship.

Anticipate joy and exhilaration as you contemplate God's thoughts. Blaise Pascal, the renowned French scientist, sought diligently to know God. The fruit of his search is expressed in some very moving lines. When he died, some of these lines were discovered written on a piece of paper he had sewn to the lining of his coat. "O righteous Father, the world hath not known Thee, but I have known Thee. Joy, joy, joy, tears of joy."

Recently, in my own paraphrasing of the Psalms, I discovered totally new thoughts to feed my heart. "You give them drink from your river of delights" (Ps. 36:8). "It was your right hand, your arm, and the light of your face, for you loved them" (Ps. 44:3).

Too seldom is God's presence a time of joy for us. Ask Him what thoughts apply to you personally and what words bring enthusiasm and joy. Or ask, "How can I embody the attitudes and trust seen in the people I've read about?" The words of Scripture can cut through our anger, enhance our confidence in Him, satisfy our emptiness. Inevitably they bring us into the presence of the Lord Jesus Himself.

If by any chance you do fall asleep, perhaps it is because, like John Bunyan's Christian, the heavy weight on your shoulders has been lifted and you are finding peace through God's Word. "Come to me, all you who are weary and burdened, and I will give you rest" (Matt. 11:28).

77

## WRAP-UP #8: GOD USES WORDS

1. What do you think Job meant when he called the Bible his necessary food?

2. Explain these two steps as they apply to reading the Bible:
a. Reproduce
b. Respond

3. Practice the three R's on a verse or paragraph of the Bible.

# PART TWO

## Today's
## Common Quandaries

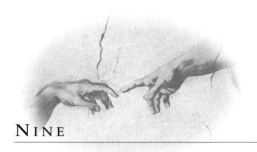

# NINE

# BIBLICALLY CORRECT ANGELS

*An angel is a spiritual creature created by God that has no physical body.*

The doorbell rang at Tony's house. He pulled himself out of his comfortable lounge chair and went to see who was there. A young man whom he did not know handed him two large pizza boxes.

"You must have the wrong house," Tony said.

"No," was the reply, "this is a present for you. It is the best, most expensive pizza we make. It's yours!"

Tony and his family were so astonished and thankful that they asked the young man to come in and enjoy the meal with them. The surprised young man kept remonstrating, but Tony's thankful spirit would not be deterred.

"We appreciate you so much. How did you know that we had very little food in the house for dinner? How did you know to choose the exact kind of pizza we like?"

Finally, the young man was able to tell the real story: "This gift of pizza was my boss's idea. He only told me to deliver it. I'm merely his messenger to bring his gift to you. He knows how much you have needed encouragement and help. Besides, he is constantly telling me what good things you are doing. He wanted to show you his love."

This fictional story of Tony and the pizza messenger illustrates our present-day misconstruction of the biblical truth about angels. In our commendable search for spirituality, we have mistakenly poured adoration and praise on the pizza delivery guy, who illustrates God's messengers: angels.

The Book of James gives us a helpful center for our laudable quest for understanding and satisfying spirituality. "Every desirable and beneficial gift comes out of heaven. The gifts are rivers of light cascading down from the Father of Light. There is nothing deceitful in God, nothing two-faced, nothing fickle. He brought us to life using the true Word, showing us off as the crown of all his creatures" (James 1:17, 18, *The Message*).

## BIBLICALLY DESCRIBED ANGELS

With the overflow of press given to angels today, we do well to see how the Bible describes them. They are mentioned more than 280 times in both the Old and New Testaments. Unlike humans, who are body and spirit, angels are incorporeal (purely spirit) beings and are given power by God to do supernatural things. "Are not all angels ministering spirits sent to serve those who will inherit salvation?" (Heb. 1:14). Hence, they are an order different than the human race, but they do not inherit salvation.

"Messenger" is the meaning of the word *angel* and neatly describes these beings. Their only contact with people is as God allows and directs them, and He alone has power over them. Some are called "angels of God," and they appear to carry out specific duties at His command. There are some differences among them in organizational rank, arranged in hierarchical order. The number of angels is probably in the millions (from Dan. 7:10). It appears evident that God created them when He created the world, for the Bible says that God "things in heaven and on earth, visible and invisible" (Col. 1:16).

There is no mention of God creating angels "in His image" nor individually, as the early chapters of Genesis record our beginning. Angels do not procreate offspring as we do (Mark 12:25). Yet they do

> **God has given His angels charge over you [Christians], to keep you in all your ways.**
>
> *Ps. 91:11*

80

have a will to obey or disobey God. Colossians 2:19 indicates that those who worship angels have lost contact with "the Head;" God.

Most importantly, the biblical description of angels never shows them as mediators between God and humans, nor are they to be worshiped. They are not pictured as more available, more compassionate, or more understanding than God Himself through Jesus Christ (1 Tim. 2:5). Wonderful blessings, promises, and gifts come from God to us, and when these come through the work of an angel, it is God who is the source. He is the Giver of life itself and the Giver of grace and mercy to us. The adoration and thanksgiving must always be to Him. Our connection is with Him, not with an angel.

## THE MEDIATOR

It is quite easy to see how angels have become a focus of praise; there is a kind of benign, loving feeling about their profile. Yet the true characteristics of God are far greater than an army of angels. Wonderful verses tell us of angels as messengers of His compassion.

"For he will command his angels concerning you to guard you in all your ways" (Ps. 91:11).

The angel of the LORD encamps around those who fear him, and he delivers them" (Ps. 34:7).

Angels are explained as seeing the face of God and are regularly in His presence. Jesus called a little child to stand with Him and then said a comforting word to the parents: "See that you do not look down on one of these little ones. For I tell you that their angels in heaven always see the face of my Father in heaven" (Matt. 18:10).

From this beautiful verse, the concept of guardian angel has been inferred. However, in all the biblical incidents involving angels, the word *guardian* is not specifically used in Scripture. The concept was adopted as a common phrase later in church history. Again, the power and help comes from God the Father.

One woman told me she had the ability to intuitively project the future, and surprisingly, her predictions frequently came through. She said she had been in touch with her own special guardian angel. I suggested there was a possibility her personality profile was strong in intuition. Then I described my own necessity to check the biblical basis and God's revealed facts with my feelings. She then asked, "But why do I have these feelings?" I could only reply that our feelings are important but may also waver, depending on other factors. Also, since the Bible does not specifically use the term "guardian angel," it is best to check all our ideas with biblical usage. This certainly is our safe reference point.

## SEE AN ANGEL?

• Angels' occupations are described in the Bible. Numerous references show angels to be praising God while in heaven and standing ready to carry out His wishes. A story in Luke 16 also tells of a beggar who died and "the angels carried him" to heaven to be with God. The prospect of angelic support carrying us to God at the time of our death I find very comforting, and it expresses God's care for us to the end.

• Angels rejoice over God's work in us. "There is rejoicing in the presence of the angels of God over one sinner who repents" (Luke 15:10). At the announcement of the birth of Jesus an angel appeared to shepherds in a field, and a great company of the "heavenly host" appeared, praising God and giving Him glory. This host is not further described in any detail, except they returned to heaven (Luke 2:9-14).

• Angels may become visible when sent by God. Our eyes are not constructed to see them ordinarily. In our everyday lives there are a number of things we know exist but cannot see: the structure of atoms, DNA, electricity, radio waves, etc. Only with special equipment do we see their effects. Biblical appearances of angels come with a specific purpose and are sent by God.

• Angels most often appear in manlike form. The Bible addresses angels in the masculine gender. This does not imply a sexual distinction as we would use the term. There is very little attempt to describe angels apart from their being sent by God as His personal spokespersons. In some Old Testament passages a being with the title "angel of the Lord" speaks for God and appears to be identified with God but is never confused with God. There is an obvious distinction.

• Only two kinds of angels are described with wings: cherubim (Gen. 3:4) and seraphim (Isa. 6:2). These are the plural form of the singular *cherub* and *seraph*. There are other references to these two, also. For centuries, popular thinking and art have given us the picture of angels with wings—a device probably used to distinguish between the angel and man.

• Gabriel and Michael are the only two angels specifically given names: Gabriel in Luke 1:26-38; Michael in Daniel 10:13 and Jude 9.

Angels do convey help as God's messengers to warn Christians of the evil so current in our world today. Billy Graham points out that "Angels spell out the tenderness of God's love, meet a pressing service; then they are gone. Angels never draw attention to themselves but ascribe glory to God and press His message upon the hearers as an urgent and sustaining word of the highest order. They are vigorous in delivering the heirs of salvation from the stratagems of evil."[20]

Our propensity as humans is to understand spiritual things by putting them in anthropomorphic terms (earthly and humanlike). This is common to all of us. Someday, when we see God face-to-face, we shall know all things more clearly. "Now we see but a poor reflection as in a mirror; then we shall see face to face," the apostle Paul says in 1 Corinthians 13:12. For the present, we have been shown the big picture: the character of God, our need for Him, and His undiluted mercy to us. Let Him be our one strong center of focus.

It is highly appropriate that we give thanks to God for His kind and willing help in our lives. God's right hand and strong arm are used frequently, as well as angels, in letting us know of His help. His care and love for us far outweigh our comprehension. His grace is beyond measure.

Since my eyes were fixed on Jesus
I've lost sight of all beside—
So enchained my spirit's vision
Looking at the Crucified.

Oh, what wonder! how amazing!
Jesus glorious King of kings,
Deigns to call me His beloved
Lets me rest beneath His wings.
　　　—John Stainer's "Crucifixion"

## WRAP-UP #9: BIBLICALLY CORRECT ANGELS

1. Reread James 1:17-18 (referred to at the beginning of this chapter). How do these words illumine the superiority of God over all other creatures?

2. When we have questions concerning angels, what steps will help our thinking?

*"Now we see but a poor reflection as in a mirror; then we shall see face to face."*
—1 Cor. 13:12

# TEN

# "THAT'S YOUR TRUTH, NOT MINE"

*A person does not call a line crooked*
*unless he or she has some idea of a straight line.*

85

Steve was one of those college students who gladden the heart of people like me. He came from a family without much interest in religion. As a child, he went with his family to church on occasion, but no one was turned on to it. As a mid-junior in university, he had one of those experiences of seeing for the first time who Jesus Christ is and said, "This is for me!" All the lights were turned on in his mind and life. No holds barred for him! Raring to go, at Christmas break he went home.

"Mom," he said as he burst through the door, "I've got to tell you. I've become a Christian."

"A Christian? Mmmmm. You always were one, right?"

"No, Mom, you don't understand. For the first time I've seen how much I really need God's help, and I prayed that God will take charge of my life."

"Oh, I see. Mmmmmm," said Mom.

Moments later Steve's dad came in the room, listened patiently to

Steve's tale, thought a moment. Then he looked Steve straight in the eye and his words came out slowly, "Steve, that may be your truth, but it's not mine." Thud!

Steve muttered under his breath something incoherent and decided he'd better go to his room to think and pray.

## MANY BELIEFS OR MANY TRUTHS?

Under the circumstances, Steve probably made a wise choice. His father's belief was different from his: "That's not my truth." He was adamant about it, tough. He seemed certain his belief was different than Steve's. He didn't say he didn't have a belief; it just wasn't the same as his son's. Actually, we all have a belief system—even the agnostic or atheist. The agnostic has a belief that we cannot know about God; the atheist has a belief that God does not exist. It is his fixed, absolute belief; it could be called his religion—his disbelief in God.

To go one step further, belief is different than truth. For instance, if I say the White House is in Peoria, that may be my belief, but you would have to look hard at reality in Peoria to find it. It cannot be verified by fact. Many beliefs do not mean many truths. Differences of opinion or beliefs is not necessarily evil in peripheral, nonessential areas. Some of these peripheral beliefs (like whether we must wear ties in church) can be held so strongly that we give them the weight of absolute truth. We have all had experiences with this.

## PREFERENCE OR VOTING?

Belief of any kind can be decided in several ways. First of all, personal preference can determine our beliefs in many diverse areas. One person prefers football, another prefers baseball. One person prefers the country to the city. One likes jazz, another the blues; one likes pumpkin pie, another likes cherry. Neither good nor bad, merely likes and dislikes. Truth is not involved in these issues, generally speaking. Second, our beliefs may be decided in more serious matters by voting: for example: tax issues, electing officials, whether the speed limit will be 65 m.p.h. In voting, of course, the majority wins.

People might try to use preference or voting to decide what is absolute truth, defined as that which conforms to reality. Both preference and voting are poor gauges for determining truth. As Ravi Zacharias says, if preference is our criteria, in some cultures they love their neighbors and in others they eat them![21] One family may prefer to be honest on their income tax; another may prefer to cheat. Truth—

and which truth we choose to follow—are at stake. Neither preference nor voting is adequate.

There are some nonreligious areas in which truth is absolute. The laws of nature are nonreversible, immutable, absolute. Recently a man jumped out of a burning building from the fourth floor and, remarkably, he did not die, but suffered multiple fractures. Gravity is not a negotiable truth, and fortunately for us, it holds our entire physical universe together, keeps the planets and the stars in their orbits. We are glad this is absolute truth!

## FACTS OR FEELINGS?

In our discussion on faith, we touched on the importance of facts and information. Absence of facts or misinterpretation of facts alters and colors our definition of truth. If we ask our four year old how much is two plus two, he might say five. His information is lacking. If he says he will always believe two plus two equals five, we tell him both four and five can't be correct. Two contradictory statements cannot both be true; this is known as the law of contradiction. If one statement is true, the opposite will be false. Dr. Zacharias also tells of two people wanting to cross the street in downtown Calcutta. One says no bus is coming; another says a bus is coming. When they cross the street, they will find out which fact is true.

**All religions can't be true because they teach opposites. Some have millions of gods, others have no gods.**

Feelings do not determine truth. We may feel something is true, but there may be quantifiable evidence to the contrary. If we feel Christianity is true today, our feelings may change about it tomorrow, depending on any number of circumstances. If we feel one religion is better than another, the question to ask is "What truth is it based on?" Absolute truth does not change. With God, areas of morals and spirituality cannot be left to preference, vote, or feelings. This is why God has revealed Himself and does not leave us to guessing.

## TRUTH: AN UNCHANGING BASE TO MEASURE BELIEFS

Without God, anything and everything is acceptable, right and wrong do not exist. In our postmodern, postrational world today, reason is banished as unnecessary. William Golding's widely read book *Lord of the Flies* described the chaos of young kids creating their own world without any guiding moral laws or conduct.[22] It didn't work! But if someone tells you truth doesn't matter, try stealing his wallet and tell him it's yours. He will demand truth!

Again, absolute truth comes from our one all-knowing God. He is our starting point, the embodiment of truth, our only unchanging, objective base for viewing ourselves and our world. Without God, we are left to preference or voting or feelings. If we do not accept God's truth as our starting point, where else can we turn?

## WHAT IS SPIRITUALITY?

Our world today is flooded with a kind of spirituality professing to provide help for our inner vacuum or hole in the soul. Anything from hugs to chicken soup is offered as a cure. Sometimes the advice and philosophy are rooted in Eastern mysticism, ethical humanism, and polytheism. The seductive "cures" are rising exponentially and give evidence of our genuine hunger and a search for helpful answers. Materialism has been the reigning king in our lives, but it has not brought the internal satisfaction we hoped for.

**Christianity is not a drug that treats some complaints.**

**It is the Truth calling out to all people.**

In the vacuum, theories and beliefs of all kinds can appear attractive and are confronting us in record numbers. Editor Lance Morrow said, "Our planet is contracting to the size of a grape." The religions of the world come in many different flavors and show us the importance of judging their validity. With any new or questionable thought, it helps to ask, "What is the truth source for the idea?"[23]

Our dedicated search for understanding is commendable. The Christian story revealed in the Bible is tailored to satisfy our minds with proven historic evidence as well as speak to our inner spiritual needs. God's truth answers our questions, satisfies our hearts, and is a verified truth source. The singular words of Jesus promise to lavishly satisfy our deepest longings. Jesus said, "I have come that they may have life, and have it to the full" (John 10:10).

## WHAT IS BIBLICALLY CORRECT SPIRITUALITY?

A few benchmarks help us define spirituality as seen in the Bible.

• God has individuality and separateness. Even as you are separate from a friend, God is separate from us and has His own individuality. He is Spirit but is real and can connect with us—mind, heart, and will. He is infinite and unlimited, yet as a person He desires to connect with each of us individually. If He were a "force," as some have claimed, we could not have a relationship with Him.

• We are not divine. Human beings are the creation of God Himself, and we need Him because we are not divine or superhuman. Although we are notably unworthy of God's grace, He gives us divine purpose for each moment of our lives. He gives us value where we are today.

• God does not bypass our minds or our wills. Connecting with God through Jesus Christ is not a paranormal experience or altered state of consciousness. God speaks truth to our hearts and minds through the Bible and through His Son, Jesus Christ. Romans 12:2 tells us He renews our minds with His Word and His thoughts.

• Morality is not relative. God is 100 percent moral and pure and has revealed His wise directions to us in the Bible. It is important to God if you ignore His wise guidance. He cares if you destroy your life by stealing someone's wife or husband, disobeying His laws, or living for self-aggrandizement. God's laws give us a life with no regrets and maximum fulfillment.

• The Christian's destiny is "paradise" in heaven. Jesus declares "Whoever believes in the Son has eternal life" (John 3:36). His words to the thief beside Him on the cross were "I tell you the truth, today you will be with me in paradise" (Luke 23:43). ("Paradise" means "the garden of God.") Heaven, the abode of God, is the destiny of the Christian; we will be with God. The apostle Paul shows us his longing for heaven: "For to me, to live is Christ and to die is gain" (Phil. 1:21).

"If I had to choose right now (to live or die), I hardly know which I'd choose. Hard choice! The desire to break camp here and be with Christ is powerful. Some days I can think of nothing better" (Phil. 1:23, *The Message*).

• Reincarnation or karma is not congruent with biblical revelation. A succession of lives aimed at ultimately gaining perfection is taught by some religions. Not only are these ideas inconsistent with

89

biblical revelation, but they are also logically untenable. If rewards and punishment through karma are intended to be a learning experience as some define it, how can those being rewarded or punished know their original state? Professor Douglas Groothuis says, "If a fifteen-year-old girl dies an agonizing death from leukemia because she was Josef Stalin in a previous life, but never knows that fact, how can that be considered just or redeeming? Or even a learning experience?"[24] (*Unmasking the New Age*).

In Jesus Christ, our truth-base is founded on the objective facts confirming His claims. He is the incarnation of God, the Creator, the one unchanging absolute truth. In the previous chapters I have related many true stories of people who have told of "getting suited up" with Jesus Christ and the difference it has made in their lives. Many more could be told. The external circumstances may differ, but the inner life change is similar. Each one has experienced an internal, personal relationship with Jesus Christ and His power to transform their life.

The future is secure for all of us who have looked up into the face of God and said, "I need Your truth for my life. I come to You through Jesus Christ and ask You to show me Your best way for my life." Instead of being engulfed by confusion, we will see a difference. He will answer.

"In him [Jesus] was life, and that life was the light of men. The light shines in the darkness, but the darkness has not understood it. … The Word became flesh and made his dwelling among us. We have seen his glory, the glory of the One and Only, who came from the Father, full of grace and truth" (John 1:4, 5, 14).

## WRAP-UP #10: "THAT'S YOUR TRUTH, NOT MINE"

1. How do truth and reason complement each other?

2. What key points help your understanding of true spirituality?

*Jesus said, "I am … the truth."*
—John 14:6

# ELEVEN

# IT'S HARD TO BE AN ATHEIST

*There was never a time when nothing existed;
otherwise nothing would exist now.*
C. S. Lewis

91

I'm really not afraid of dogs, but every time I enter the Johnsons'
home, I steel myself for the overpowering and uncontrollable welcome
from their oversized black Lab. As usual, any two of the family available pull valiantly on the dog's leash, simultaneously screaming
"Down! Buster! Down, Buster." After I successfully navigate through
the door, as quickly as possible I reach for Buster's neck and begin the
routine scratching to which he is accustomed.

From Buster's rapacious appetite for attention, one could justifi-
ably conclude he has the same intelligence and interpersonal understanding as his scholarly owners. However, there's a distinct cutoff
point. I have never heard him ask, "Who am I?" or "Why am I here?"
or "Is there a God?" Nor does he ever ask, "Is my behavior good or
bad, right or wrong?"

It has been said that no animal has ever been observed building a
cathedral. What is the difference? Are human beings, in all of their
complexity, just accidents in a mechanistic universe? Could some

minor difference in form and chemical ingredients have made Buster into a person instead of a dog? Or even given him the capacity to operate a computer?

These questions have been debated among philosophers and thinkers for centuries. The oft-quoted Frederick Nietzsche opined that if God is dead, man is dead. Logic and common sense cause us to question both of these assertions. Let's pose some questions about who we are as a human race and what our origins were.

1. Are we merely glorified animals?

2. Are we an accident of history floating on the sea of life without meaning?

3. Are we cogs in an impersonal, deterministic universe?

4. Is our origin totally impersonal, with no personal God at our beginning?

5. Did we complex creatures evolve as a result of time (billions of years) plus chance plus the right congruence of chemicals?

The atheist would doubtless answer "Yes" to all of the above. According to that worldview, we are glorified animals, accidents of history. Each life is but a coalescence of chemicals evolving over billions of years from a primordial soup. (Where did the soup come from?) With these beliefs, the atheist is making his personal "truth statements" as he sees them. The inference is that the difference between a human being and a tree is solely in form and complexity. Love, choice, morals, aesthetics are but chemical reactions.

> **God made the tree, but He is not the tree. He is the Creator.**

If the origin of life is impersonal then no one is at home in the universe, and humans are highly efficient machines. Relationships and words will evaporate for want of any significance. Not an enticing picture. It is hard to be an atheist!

## NOTHING PRODUCES NOTHING

To the question, "Does God exist and is He a reality?" our frame of reference is the world we see and experience. We know we are alive and we experience a mind-reeling world around us. We cannot rationally deny our own or our world's existence. It is something, not nothing! Therefore, we conclude someone or something produced it and us. Somehow it all had a beginning; indeed, everything had a beginning. Nothing produces nothing.

Theories about "first causes" or origins have filled volumes since recorded history. If we discover a fine painting at our front door, our first question is, where did it originate? Who might be the kind donor? Lack of information doesn't erase the fact that someone made it and brought it to the door. There is an effect. What was the cause? "Nothing" would not be an explanation.

Whitaker Chambers, famed double agent for the Communists during the Cold War, in his book *Witness* wrote of seeing the fallacy in atheism and turning himself in to authorities. Sometime afterward, he watched his infant child in a high chair and wondered at the intricacy of her small ear. Seeing the artistry of its design moved him to conclude for the first time that there had to be a very skilled Creator who made it.[25]

The entire human body is a wonder. The intricate design of the eye brought Albert Einstein to say he was almost moved to believe in a divine Designer. The brain mystifies even the most learned. One hundred thousand billion electrical connections compose each person's brain, at last count. That exceeds more than all the electrical connections in every electrical appliance in the entire world! Did this mysterious brain evolve by itself? That defies credulity. Countless similar examples from biology, astronomy, and every facet of cosmology point to a Cause beyond what we observe—a very powerful and talented Cause.

If no Creator God exists, could we accept the conclusion that *nothing* brought this universe and us into existence? That would be hard!

## DESIGN AND INFORMATION

In our everyday world, we accept automatically both simple and complex things, and all presuppose a designer. The TV set did not start with an electrical cord and a socket. It began with a design, a plan. A tract of new houses is built, but it all started with a mind, a drawing board, and an individual who drew up a blueprint.

Examples abound of intriguing mysteries in our universe. Scientists in recent years, with the help of improved microscopes and other instruments, have unraveled RNA and DNA in the laboratory, the design installed by the divine Artist in the very beginning. Our world reflects unequaled plan and wisdom, as well as an active mind who provided the information. Even if we waited for infinite time and infinite chance, as the evolutionist suggests, would a world so meticulous evolve? Design and information must precede any creative actions. A divine Creator would be needed to get the action started.

Our world and its intricate design have shown the plausibility of God's existence. He does exist objectively, regardless of what we think. I dare to say this dogmatically, not because of some psychic intelligence, but because of the powerful evidence of nature, the fine-tunedness of the cosmos. It is interesting to note that there is a God consciousness in even the most primitive of cultures.

G. K. Chesterton said, "The sun does not rise because of the rotation of the earth. The sun rises because God says to it, 'Get up.'" God the Creator actively keeps our cosmos working, discloses His power and glory, His character and personality, His will and His ways.

It's interesting to note that modern science, with its laws of uniformity, was founded by committed Christians. These early scientists rejected the conclusions of Greek polytheistic notions and viewed the Creator as a God of order and not caprice. Surely these early scientists would reject the atheistic view of mechanistic naturalism common today. They believed this world God had made was intended to be explored, could be understood and enjoyed by man. A recent *Time* magazine article entitled "How Life Began" ended with "For all the scientific discoveries and fancy equipment, scientists have yet to produce anything in a test tube that would shake a faith in God. The more scientists learn, the more extraordinary life seems. Progress in understanding the origin of life should ultimately enhance, not diminish the wonder of it."[26]

Romans 1:20 plausibly says, "For since the creation of the world God's invisible qualities—his eternal power and divine nature—have been clearly seen, being understood from what has been made."

## INVISIBILITY NOT A MYSTERY

God's invisible presence and His visible creation were made known to His creatures at the very beginning. Understandably, we depend on visibility for most of our lives. Yet we also rely on many things we cannot see. Electricity and radio waves we've already mentioned. Human qualities such as beauty, love, character, even our own inner spirits, are invisible, yet we accept these without question. We also accept mind and will, as well as ethics, aesthetics, and morals. All invisible.

God's invisibility, we have said previously, does not mean that He is unreal.

## THE CUTOFF POINT

The eternal, personal God created the universe. In chapter 1 of Genesis we're given the following sequence:

Light
Air and water
Dry land
Vegetation
Moon and stars
Birds and fish
Animals

Then the Creator made a distinct cutoff point. Unlike anything God had created before, He created a man and woman, each described as made in His own image—God's own moral image (Gen. 1:27). None of His other creations had this distinction. There were dinosaurs, chimpanzees, whales, birds, and many other creatures, but none were given God's moral image.

This stamp of God's image sets you and me and the whole human race apart from all the rest of creation. He honored us with an intrinsically special value. This new kind of creature with God's image was made to comprehend God's mind and heart. When God told them "Thou shalt not," the man and woman understood His words.

> An atheist doesn't find God for the same reason a thief doesn't find a policeman. He is not looking for Him.

## WHAT IS A MORAL IMAGE?

• First, God's moral image gave us humans built-in comprehension of right and wrong. It's an intuitive knowledge, called a moral "ought" or a conscience, and it comes with us at birth. All of us have a knowing inside, whispering to us that one choice is right and another choice is wrong. God's image in us loves good and hates evil and differentiates between the two. The Bible sometimes also refers to this faculty as the conscience.

• Second, we know we are distinct from God, distinct from each other. Each person carries an individual personality apart from God and apart from every other creature in the world. I am not God, and God is not me. Likewise, I am not you, and you are not me.

95

• Third, each person is responsible for personal actions and choices, right or wrong. Furthermore, human beings were given a supreme place in the cosmos. They were told to possess the earth and make it serve them. "Rule over ... every living creature," they were told (Gen. 1:28).

Our God-given moral image and conscience define us as human, not animal. If there were no image of God within us, morality would be a miracle, standards unnecessary, and an honest person a fool.

## THE WONDER OF GOD'S GLORY

"In the beginning God" are the first four words of the Bible (Gen. 1:1). God was the initiator of our physical world and its people. His actions and His personality form the single strand that flows through the Bible, from beginning to end. It traces God's teaching and discloses His will to the people He created. The climax of this strand of history culminates in God's sending a personal Savior for us.

The writer to Hebrews puts it, "In the past God spoke to our forefathers through the prophets at many times and in various ways, but in these last days he has spoken to us by His Son [Jesus Christ]" (Heb. 1:1, 2). Today, we can speak of "knowing God" through Jesus Christ and possessing a certainty that He hears and answers. Those who saw Jesus on earth caught a glimpse of God in the flesh, and by His Spirit, we too can see God's glory in Jesus Christ. "For God, who said, 'Let light shine out of darkness,' made his light shine in our hearts to give us the light of the knowledge of the glory of God in the face of Jesus Christ" (2 Cor. 4:6).

**Did the God who endowed us with reason intend us to forgo its usage? God calls out: "Come now, let us reason together...."**

*Isa. 1:18*

• God's love for us is infinite. It is directed toward us. The dictionary defines infinite as "without limits," beyond any measurements we could obtain. God's infinite love far exceeds any finite equivalent. The biblical description is couched in phrases like these:

> "For as high as the heavens are above the earth, so
> great is his love for those who fear him" (Ps. 103:11).

"I have loved you with an everlasting love" (Jer. 31:3).

"I led them with cords of human kindness, with ties of love" (Hos. 11:4).

"In his love and mercy he redeemed them" (Isa. 63:9).

"This is love: not that we loved God, but that he loved us" (1 John 4:10).

• God's love has been indescribably costly to Him. In any relationship the cost to the giver of love demonstrates the depth, degree, and kind of love offered. A person who scrimps, saves, and sacrifices for the family is expressing love for them. A person who takes a second job to get enough money to send a child to college does it for love of that child. It costs time and energy. Parents who organize their schedules so they can be home for dinner are showing love for their family.

No verse in the Bible is as expressive of the enormous cost of God's love than Jesus' words in John 3:16: "For God so loved the world that he gave his one and only Son [Jesus]." Who of us would sacrifice one of our children for someone known to us, let alone for someone who has scarcely acknowledged us? The New Testament Book of Romans says it succinctly, "God demonstrates his own love for us in this: While we were still sinners, Christ died for us" (Rom. 5:8).

• God's love is constant and stable, not volatile like human love. "Yesterday I loved you; tomorrow I may not." A friend told me his wife would love him if he dangled some bauble before her; if not, he said, she is "cold as ice." This is human love, totally unlike divine love. God's love is of an entirely different caliber. In the biblical verses quoted above, God's love is intentional and fixed toward us, without any spiritual makeup or perfume. After all, He has engraved each of us with His image.

• God's love is strong and sturdy like a cedar tree (as Psalm 29 describes Him) and will not be shaken by inconsistencies He sees in us or changes in our attitudes toward Him. He will wait for us to call on Him, to lean on Him.

This is a God who lives, who has revealed Himself to us and is worth trusting with our entire life!

## WRAP-UP #11: IT'S HARD TO BE AN ATHEIST

1. How does the phrase "nothing produces nothing" show the reasonableness of believing in God's existence?

2. Review these four attributes of God's love and explain them in your own words:

   a. Infinite
   b. Costly
   c. Constant
   d. Strong

*"How great is the love the Father has lavished on us."*
—1 John 3:1

# PART THREE

# *Magnificent Staying Power*

# STAYING POWER
# FOR THE JOURNEY

*S*eeking God is worth putting everything
else aside to find Him.

A man was digging in a field when suddenly his shovel made a
loud clank. He hit something hard. He turned the soil over and found
a valuable treasure worth more than he had ever dreamed of. The man
was overcome with jubilation and quickly covered up his find with the
soil. He dashed home and sold everything he had. Then he bought the
whole field to acquire the treasure (Matt. 13:44).

Another man was searching for fine pearls. He scoured the world,
and he uncovered a pearl of exquisite beauty and rare value. This was
a once-in-a-lifetime find. He, too, sold everything he had and bought
the pearl of great price (Matt. 13:45).

One day, as the customary crowd followed Jesus Christ, He spun
these tales of two men who, in their life journeys, found the ultimate
riches, a treasure and a pearl. Jesus started both stories with the phrase
"The kingdom of heaven is like ... " With this introduction, there is
no doubt the audience would want to hear more.

Jesus was explaining that God's kingdom is the greatest "treasure" and brings life's most magnificent connection. The entire life of Jesus and the whole of the Bible center on this. It is not about money; it is about gaining life's most valuable goal: to know God Himself, personally. It would be hard to dream up a goal that surpasses this one!

Eric Liddell, the Olympic runner whose entire life was connected to God, said, "I feel God's pleasure when I run." Johann Sebastian Bach wrote the music to an anthem starting with the words "Jesus, priceless treasure, source of purest pleasure, truest friend to me." Both of these men found the true treasure.

In my teen years, as a new Christian, and sensing for the first time the treasure of forgiveness and a worthwhile goal for life, I discovered an unbeatable promise. It tells me of "the God of all grace" and adds, Jesus Christ Himself will "perfect, stablish, strengthen, settle you" (1 Pet. 5:10, KJV). I needed this assurance and continued to pore over the Bible, wanting to know more and more about this priceless treasure. For all of us, we bring nothing when we come to Jesus, and we gain the incomparable connection.

## TWO KINDS OF LOOKING

The two men in Jesus' stories looked for treasure in two different ways, Jesus implied. The first man accidentally discovered a treasure in a field. He may have plowed the same field hundreds of times before, but this time, in the normal, everyday digging, he hit something unusual. In our journeys, we may fall into this accidental category, not even looking for God. Then some desperate circumstance or grinding habit unearths our need for Him. The death of a loved one, financial reverses, or injustice from others can move us to reach out and seek connection with Jesus Christ, the ultimate treasure.

The second man searched intentionally. It is possible this merchant scoured the few places in the world where pearls might be hidden. He knew he needed to seek diligently, and his search was rewarded. Both of these men sold everything they had to secure the treasure.

Recently I talked to a young man the very night he began his relationship with Jesus Christ. He told me he had spent the week before checking out a list of religions in his area, even looking in the phone book and calling religious organizations. This young man, and the man in Jesus' story, kept pursuing until they found the pearl of great price. And each of them was filled with exultant joy. Seeking God is worth putting everything else aside to find Him.

"Ask and it will be given to you; seek and you will find; knock and the door will be opened to you" (Matt. 7:7).

## THE PRODIGAL SON STORY

This story, in Luke 15:11-32, has been called by some the greatest story in the world. Here, Jesus tells the true-to-life account of a younger son, who has come to be known as the Prodigal Son. The young man boldly asked his father for his share of the family estate. We can guess the son was chafing under his father's restrictions and structure. He thought he would be happy far away. According to Jewish practice, giving a younger son his inheritance early was highly unusual. The young man seemed oblivious to his father's needs and desires. Surprisingly, the father gave him his inheritance.

What was in this young man's mind? What motivated his action? No doubt he began to hear some grandly built-up stories about a far country, the bright lights, the fun, absence of restraints from parents, lack of moral or social restrictions. He may have even heard that he would find more love far away. We could let our imagination run. Perhaps he thought the lights would be brighter and life away from his father's house far better. In some ways we can relate to this, too. We can easily think life would be better if only our circumstances would change!

**Connecting with God through Jesus Christ enables the weak to remain strong. Magnificent!**

103

In the end, of course, the young man discovered he was deceived; this was not the secret to happiness. He had believed the lie that life would be trouble-free out in the world. After spending all his money, he ended up feeding pigs as well as eating their food. The very worst thing one could imagine for a Jewish man would be working and eating in a pig pen, given the Jewish teaching that pigs were unclean animals.

Finally, the young fellow saw the truth and reality and became desperate. He turned and started toward home to his father. While he was still a long way off, the waiting father saw him approaching and was overwhelmed with compassion for him. He ran out to his son, flung his arms around his neck, and kissed him tenderly. The son's first words were "Father, I have sinned against heaven and you. I am no longer worthy to be called your son; make me like one of your hired men" (vv. 18–19).

But his father could not contain his excitement. His son had returned and their connection was restored! His longed-for day had come! He called his friends together to celebrate. He gave his son a new robe, a ring for his finger, shoes for his feet, love, and a big welcome party with the best food. The story closes in verse 32 with these moving words from the father to the older brother, "This brother of yours was dead and is alive again; he was lost and is found."

"The Waiting Father": This was the title given to Jesus' story by theologian Helmut Thielicke. What a welcome for a runaway son, and what a graphic picture of the heart of the welcoming father! The waiting father was the hero; he never gave up watching for his son to come home. He portrays how God, our Savior and our Hero, waits for us to turn and come home to Him. His persevering love draws us irresistibly to Him, and His grace and His kindness are unmatched. This is finding the kingdom of God and the eternally safe presence of the Waiting Father.

> A safe question for us in any decision is: "What would Jesus do?"

John Donne said, "One of the most convenient hieroglyphics of God is a circle; and a circle is endless; whom God loves he loves to the end."[27] The divine waiting Father stays with us. He will never leave us until the very end of our lives.

104

## STAYING POWER

In the security of the heavenly Father's presence we find a staying power for our lives. Being connected brings steadiness and endurance; we need His staying power. Life for all of us may bring changes in both circumstances and people—change happens to everyone. Turning to and trusting God and staying with Him is the most valid, secure resting place.

This security and safety in the Father's house is not a blind, inexorable fate (such as that called kismet in Islam). No, this is the supreme Creator God who knows us individually and loves us with an everlasting love. Our connection is magnificent and our staying power comes from Him. He empowers us to stand firm to the end as Jesus promised (Matt. 24:13; Mark. 13:13). The apostle Paul said he had learned to be content and do everything "through him who gives me strength" (Phil. 4:13). All the advantages of God's constant companionship, direction, guidance, and forgiveness are ours. As with any relationship, we can come to know Him better and better over time.

"His divine power has given us everything we need for life and godliness through our knowledge of him who called us by his own glory and goodness" (2 Pet. 1:3).

Two practical suggestions for life's journey:

• First, pursue God and His kingdom energetically. Intentional effort to learn His Word and expand our inner connection with Him will be rewarded. When the prodigal arrived home, he was close to his father, with all the benefits of that close relationship. God will direct us and wants to be our driver! If all we are doing is staring at a road map or staying parked in the garage of life, the kingdom of God will be less than meaningful to us. God leads us as we specifically, inch by inch, pursue His will and expand our lives to the maximum.

• Second, apply the Scripture to everyday life. If we feed our minds with God's perspective and check the Bible for God's words, we will find truths that apply to our circumstances. Try to make this a daily habit. Are there any examples in Jesus' life we might imitate? Acquiring revealed truths and answers to questions lays a solid base for our staying power. Check your old, ineffective thinking patterns; be open to making some changes, if necessary. Ask how a new truth can fit into your everyday living. Recall the phrase "new life" and learn the biblical contrast with the "old life" (Eph. 4:22–24). Connect with other Christians in church and Bible studies. This will enhance the learning and root out answers to questions.

Remember, the downturn in the prodigal's life began in his mind, not in his feet! He believed the old, groundless stories and allowed himself to become star-struck by all he heard. Then his feet began to act on these new ideas. He got up, left home, and ended up with the pigs.

Our actions (and our emotions) are rooted in our thinking. Unknowingly, most of us accept uncritically the mindset of our culture: the outlook conveyed by books, movies, TV, magazines, pictures, and perhaps our friends. Our core self can be darkened or lightened, depending on what we allow into our minds. Based on poor trendy ideas and moods, life-altering decisions can topple us.

By contrast, God's thoughts give us the very groundwork for living every day as one belonging to the kingdom of God. The Bible and the Holy Spirit living within us are His instruments and give us His input for our mind and emotions.

An old saying is "We can't keep the birds from flying around our heads, but we can keep them from making a nest in our hair." The more

God's thoughts are "nested in our hair," the stronger our inner life grows. Romans 12:2 uses the phrase "be transformed by the renewing of your mind." Godly transformation begins in the mind.

## NO HALFWAY TURNS

The men in Jesus' first two stories turned their lives around 100 percent. They entertained no second thoughts, no grumbling or secret compromise to pay only half price for their finds. The two men gleefully gave up all they had! Even their most valuable possessions didn't compare a tad with the prize they had gained. Turning was a hilarious act full of joy and expectation.

If we get the urge to go only halfway (keep a little back) in seeking the Lord, it is time to check our focus. The Prodigal Son might have said, "I'll stay at my father's house, but my heart is still out with the boys and doing my own thing." This would be halfway coming home, halfway returning to his father. When it comes to placing faith in Jesus Christ, there is no halfway.

That would be like saying, "I'll be halfway married." It's impossible, and those who have tried it predictably see the relationship collapse. A true spouse values the relationship and the person above all others. In marriage each partner leaves all others and cleaves to only one. Similarly, straddling the fence between ourselves and the God of heaven, between His way and ours, between good and evil will not work. Could the Prodigal Son bring home a pan of pig food and offer it to the father? Of course not.

## FOLLOW HIM HARD

I have found help in the baseline thought: follow Him hard. We "offer ourselves" to Him without compromise. As a young Christian, I wanted to hold on to a successful job, money, education, marriage, and family, yet God had some other things to teach me. These involved things like giving Him some of my old broken ideas, my present circumstances, my personality, and most importantly, my entire future.

Gradually some light began to filter into my brain. He wanted me to know for certain that He was more than capable of taking care of my today and my tomorrow—far better than I could. We can trust Him with the unknowns of the future. Because God is God, He is infinitely wise, powerful, and loving.

When my child comes to me and tells me he loves me, I don't respond with, "Great, stay in your room for three weeks with only bread and water." Of course not. I melt inside. Nor is God's response meager when we tell Him we will return and follow Him hard. Our hearts will be engulfed by His love.

Does this mean the absence of problems? Of course not. It does mean we recognize Jesus Christ is with us in every circumstance of life. Like many others, I have learned more of God's love for me while going through difficulties than in the relatively calm times. Some of these lessons I would never have learned without hardship. Malcolm Muggeridge, toward the end of his life, said, "The only worthwhile things I learned in life were through suffering."[28]

> **Only God is permanently interesting. Other things we may fathom, but He out-tops our thoughts.**

### REPLACEMENT THEORY

Following Him hard is putting into action what I call the replacement theory. Whenever our negative, all-consuming passions return (and we all have them), our new love, Jesus Christ Himself, can replace the damaging patterns with His wisdom and power. We must replace the worries and obsessions and focus on Him. Then our relationship becomes one of reciprocal love.

"What would Jesus do?" is a reliable question to use for replacing any negative attitudes or activities. It can be a reminder that He is there with us and will help. A young friend who had deviant sexual obsessions used the reminder "When I close the bedroom door with someone, I know Jesus goes in with us. I don't want to end up in the pig pen."

The heavenly Father is walking with us on our journey. He is waiting for us with a welcoming party.

> "Come, all you who are thirsty, come to the waters; and you who have no money, come, buy and eat!" (Isa. 55:1).

> "Seek the LORD while he may be found; call on him while he is near" (Isa. 55:6).

> "You will go out in joy and be led forth in peace" (Isa. 55:12).

> "'You will seek me and find me when you seek me with all our heart. I will be found by you,' declares the LORD" (Jer. 29:13-14).

## WRAP-UP #12: STAYING POWER FOR THE JOURNEY

1. From the stories of the treasure and the priceless pearl, what attitude does God want us to have toward Him and His kingdom?

2. How does the story of the Prodigal Son inspire and reassure you in your relationship with God?

3. If you were to "follow Jesus hard," what differences would that mean in your life?

*Pray to the Lord! Ask Him what He wants you to remember and integrate into your life from the foregoing pages.*

## NOTES

**Chapter 1: *Inner Direction Needed***

1. John Donne, *We Lie Down in Hope* (Elgin, Ill.: David C. Cook Publishing Co., 1977), 41.

2. John Hiatt, "Is Anybody There?" (Hollywood, Calif.: A & M Records, 1988).

3. Martyn Lloyd-Jones, *Joy Unspeakable* (Wheaton, Ill.: Shaw Publishers, 1984).

4. Kevin Graham Ford, *Jesus for a New Generation* (Downers Grove, Ill.: InterVarsity Press, 1994) 256, quoting Douglas Coupland, *Life After God*.

5. Helmut Thielicke, *Living Quotations for Christians* (New York: Harper & Row, 1974), 92.

**Chapter 2: *Jesus Christ, the Centerpiece***

6. Article in *Chicago Tribune* referring to *Not by Bread Alone*; Vladimir Dudintsev, c1957.

7. *The Bridges of Madison County*, film review by Douglas W. Kmiec, (Chicago, Ill., *Chicago Tribune*, June 9, 1995), 27.

**Chapter 3: *Alone on the Stage of History***

8. Malcolm Muggeridge, *Jesus, the Man Who Lives* (New York: Harper & Row), 1992, 9.

9. Helmut Thielicke, *The Waiting Father* (New York: Harper & Row) 1959.

**Chapter 4: *Love and Justice Meet***

10. John Bunyan, *The Pilgrim's Progress* (New York: P. F. Collier & Son, 1969), 196.

11. G. K. Chesterton,

12. Ravi Zacharias, *Just Thinking; The Court of Last Resort*, (Norcross, GA, RZIM, 1996), 4.

**Chapter 5: *He's Alive***

13. David Strauss, *The Life of Jesus for the People*, 2d ed. (London, 1879), 1:412.

**Chapter 6: *Jesus Christ, a Valid Object***

14. C. S. Lewis, *Surprised by Joy*, (San Diego, New York, London: Harcourt Brace & Co. 1956), 224 f.

**Chapter 7: *Making the Magnificent Connection***

15. C. S. Lewis, *Mere Christianity*, (Westwood, N.J.: Barbour Co., 1952), 134–136.

16. John Stott, *Basic Christianity*, (Chicago, Ill., InterVarsity Press, 1964), 126.

**Chapter 8: *God Uses Words***

17. Sir William Ramsey, *Archaeology and Bible History*, (Wheaton, Ill.: Scripture Press Publications, 1969), 317.

18. *Servant Magazine*, World Update (Three Hills, Alberta, 2001), 9.

19. Ibid., Lloyd-Jones, 106.

**Chapter 9: *Biblically Correct Angels***

20. Billy Graham, *Angels*, (Word, Dallas, 1995), 25.

Chapter 10: *"That's Your Truth, Not Mine"*

    21. Ravi Zacharias, *Can Man Live Without God?* (Dallas: Word, 1994), 182.

    22. William Golding, *Lord of the Flies*, (New York: Coward-McCann, 1962).

    23. Lance Morrow, "Hooray For Bill Gates, I Guess", *Time*, Jan.13, 1997, 84.

    24. Douglas R. Groothuis, *Unmasking the New Age*, (Downers Grove, Ill.: InterVarsity Press, 1986), 150.

Chapter 11: *It's Hard to Be an Atheist*

    25. Whittaker Chambers, *Witness*, (New York: Random House, 1962).

    26. Madeleine Nash, "How Life Began," *Time*, Oct. 11, 1993.

Chapter 12: *Staying Power for the Journey*

    27. John Donne, *Living Quotations for Christians*, 87.

    28. Malcolm Muggeridge, quoted in Donald McCullough, *Waking from the American Dream*, (Downers Grove, Ill.: InterVarsity Press, 1988), 145.

# Providing Answers for the Next Generation—
## *More Classics by Paul E. Little*

## Know Why You Believe

You're a reasonable person. And you know there are some tough questions that Christianity should be able to answer. Paul Little does just that, and in a way that Billy Graham lauds as "scholarly, articulate," and yet "simple." Revised and expanded to explore the central truths of Christianity in a more contemporary format, this companion bestseller examines the claims of the Christian faith. Discover for yourself what such great Christian minds as Bill Hybels, Josh McDowell, and Ravi Zacharias have found to be a must-have classic for any critical thinker's library.

**ISBN:** 0-78143-963-9   ITEM #: 102856
Format:  PB    Size 5-1/2 x 8-1/2    Pages: 160

## Know What You Believe

You're a Christian—but what does that really mean?  Do you know and understand God's Word and the doctrines of the Christian faith?  Walk through the essentials with Paul Little in this companion bestselling classic, revised and expanded to explore the central truths of Christianity in a more contemporary format.

**ISBN:** 0-78143-964-7   ITEM #: 102857
Format:  PB    Size 5-1/2 x 8-1/2    Pages: 160

### Order your copies today!
### Order online: www.cookministries.com
### Phone: 1-800-323-7543
### Or visit your local Christian bookstore.